the Younger Pliny, William Melmoth

The Letters of Pliny the Consul

With Occasional Remarks. Edition 9, Vol. II

the Younger Pliny, William Melmoth

The Letters of Pliny the Consul
With Occasional Remarks. Edition 9, Vol. II

ISBN/EAN: 9783744716987

Printed in Europe, USA, Canada, Australia, Japan

Cover: Foto ©Thomas Meinert / pixelio.de

More available books at **www.hansebooks.com**

THE
LETTERS
OF
PLINY
THE
CONSUL:

With Occasional REMARKS.

By WILLIAM MELMOTH, Esq;

THE NINTH EDITION,
REVISED AND CORRECTED.

VOL. II.

LONDON:
Printed for J. DODSLEY, in Pall-Mall.
M.DCC.XCVI.

THE LETTERS OF *PLINY.*

BOOK VII.

LETTER I. *To* RESTITUTUS.

THIS obstinate distemper which hangs upon you, greatly alarms me; and tho' I know how extremely temperate you are, yet I am afraid your disease should get the better of your moderation. Let me intreat you then to resist it with a determined abstemiousness: a remedy, be assured, of all others the most laudable, as well as the most salutary. There is nothing impracticable in what I recommend: it is a rule, at least, which I always enjoin

enjoin my family to observe with respect to myself. I tell them, should I be attacked with any disorder, I hope I shall desire nothing of which I ought either to be ashamed, or have reason to repent; however, if my distemper should prevail over my judgement, I forbid them to give me any thing but by the consent of my physicians; and I assure the people about me, that I shall resent their compliance with me in things improper, as much as another man would their refusal. I had once a most violent fever; when the fit was a little abated, and I had been anointed[a], my physician offered me something to drink: I desired he would first feel my pulse; and upon his seeming to think the paroxysm was not quite abated I instantly returned the cup, tho' it was just at my lips. Afterwards, when I was preparing to go into the bath, twenty days from the first attack of my illness, perceiving the physicians whispering together, I enquired what they were saying. They replied, they were of opinion I might possibly bathe with safety, nevertheless that they were not without some suspicion of hazard. What occasion then is there,

---

[a] Unction was much esteemed as a remedy in certain cases by the ancient physicians. Celsus, who flourished, it is supposed, about Pliny's time, expressly recommends it in the remission of acute distempers: *ungi leniterque pertractari corpus, etiam in acutis et recentibus morbis oportet; in remissione tamen,* &c. Celsi med. ed. Almeloveen, p. 88.

there, I afked, of bathing at all? And thus, with great complacency, I gave up a pleasure I was upon the point of enjoying, and abstained from the bath with the same satisfaction I was preparing to enter it. I mention this, not only in order to enforce my advice by example; but also that this letter may be a sort of tie upon me to observe the same resolute abstinence for the future. Farewel.

LETTER II. *To* JUSTUS.

ARE you not inconsistent, when you assure me you have no intermission from business, and yet express at the same time an earnest desire to see my works; upon which even the idle will scarce bestow some of their useless hours? I will not then break in upon your occupations during this summer season; but when the return of winter shall make it probable that your evenings, at least, may be disengaged, I will look over my trifles for something to amuse your vacant hours. In the mean while, I shall be well satisfied, if my letters should not prove troublesome; as I suspect they are, and therefore shorten them. Farewel.

LETTER III. *To* Præsens.

ARE you determined then to pass your whole time between [a] Lucania and [b] Campania? Your answer, I suppose, will be, that the former is your native country, and the latter that of your wife. This, I admit, may justify a long absence, but I cannot allow it as a reason for a perpetual one. But are you resolved in good earnest never to return to Rome; that theatre of honours, preferment, and amicable connections of every sort? Are you obstinately determined to live your own master; to sleep as long as you please, and to rise when you think proper? Will you never change your country garb for the dress of the town, but spend your whole days unembarrassed by our crowded streets? It is time, however, you should re-visit this our scene of hurry, were it only that your rural pleasures may not grow languid by uninterrupted possession: appear at the levees of the great, that you may enjoy the same honour yourself with the more satisfaction; and mix in our crowds, that you may have a keener relish for the charms of solitude. But am I not imprudently retarding the friend I would recall? It is these very circumstances, perhaps,

[a] Comprehending the Basilicata, a province in the kingdom of Naples.
[b] Now called Campagna di Roma. See B. vi. let. 4. not. [b].

haps, that induce you every day more and more to seclude yourself up in retirement. All however I wish to prevail with you is, only to intermit, not to renounce the charms of solitude. If I were to invite you to a feast, as I would blend dishes of a poignant taste, with those of the luscious kind, in order to sharpen the edge of your palate by the one, which had been flattened by the other; so I now advise you to enliven sometimes the smooth pleasures of life, with those of a more active nature. Farewel.

LETTER IV. *To* PONTIUS.

YOU have read, it seems, my poems, and are desirous to know, how it happened that a man of my gravity (as you are pleased to call me, tho' in truth, I am only not a trifler) could adopt this mode of composition. To take the account then a good way back, I must acquaint you that I had always an inclination to poetry, insomuch that when I was fourteen years of age, I composed a Tragedy in Greek. If you should ask me what sort of one? I protest I don't know; all that I remember of it is, that it was called a Tragedy. Some time afterwards, in my return from the army, being detained in the island of ᵃ Icaria by contrary winds,

---

ᵃ An island in the Archipelago, now called Nicaria.

winds, I vented my spleen against that place in some Latin Elegies. I have since made some attempts in the heroic kind; but these *Hendecasyllables* are the first I ever composed in that measure: and the following accident gave birth to them. The treatise of Asinius Gallus was read to me one day at Laurentinum, wherein he draws a comparison between his father and Cicero; and cites an epigram of Tully's on his favourite Tiro. Upon retiring to take my afternoon's nap (for it was summer) and not being able to sleep, I began to reflect that the greatest orators have been fond of poetry, and valued themselves upon it. I tried therefore what I could do in this way; and tho' I had long disused myself to compositions of this nature, I struck out, in a much shorter time than I could have imagined, the following lines upon the subject which gave me the first hint:

> *When Gallus I read, who pretends that his sire*
> *Had far more than Tully poetical fire,*
> *The wisest of men, I perceiv'd held it fit*
> *To temper his wisdom with love and with wit;*
> *For Tully, grave Tully, in amorous strains,*
> *Of the frauds of his paramour Tiro complains;*
> *That faithless to love, and to pleasure untrue,*
> *From his promis'd embrace the arch wanton withdrew.*

Then

ᵇ See p. 217. note ᵃ.

Then I said to my heart, Why shouldst thou conceal
The sweetest of passions, the love which you feel—
Yes, fly wanton muse, and proclaim it around,
Thy Pliny has lov'd, and his Tiro has found;
The coy one so artful, who sweetly denies,
And from the soft flame, but to heighten it, flies.

From this I turned to Elegy, which flowed from me with the same ease; and being thus drawn in by the facility with which the Muses yielded to my addresses, I proceeded to encrease the number of my productions of this kind. At my return to Rome, I shewed my performances to some of my friends, who were pleased to approve of them. Afterwards, whenever I had leisure, and particularly when I travelled, I made several other attempts in the poetical way. At length I determined, after the example of many others, to publish a separate volume of these poems; and I have no reason to repent of my resolution. They are much enquired after, and are in every body's hands; they have even tempted the Greeks to learn our language, who sing them to their harps and lyres. But will you not imagine I begin to rave? remember, however, poets have that privilege. The truth is, I am not giving you my own judgment, but that of others, which, be it right or wrong, I am much pleased with; and have only to wish that posterity may be of the same opinion. Farewel.

LETTER V. *To* CALPHURNIA[a].

IT is incredible how impatiently I wish for your return; such is the tenderness of my affection for you, and so unaccustomed am I to a separation! I lie awake the greatest part of the night in thinking of you, and (to use a very common, but very true expression) my feet carry me of their own accord to your apartment, at those hours I used to visit you; but not finding you there, I return with as much sorrow and disappointment as an excluded lover. The only intermission my anxiety knows, is when I am engaged at the bar, and in the causes of my friends. Judge then, how wretched must *his* life be, who finds no repose but in *business*; no consolation but in a *crowd*. Farewel.

LETTER VI. *To* MACRINUS.

A Very singular and remarkable circumstance has happened in the affair of [b] Varenus; the consequence of which is yet in suspense. The Bithynians, it is *said*, (for I only mention it as a report) have dropped their prosecution of him; being, it seems convinced at last, that the accusation was extremely ill founded. A deputy from that province

[a] His wife. [b] See B. v. let. xx.

province is arrived, who has brought with him a decree of their assembly; copies of which he has delivered to Cæsar, and to several of the principal persons in Rome, as also to us the advocates for Varenus. 'Magius, nevertheless, whom I mentioned in my last letter, persists in his charge; to support which, he is incessantly teazing the worthy Nigrinus. This excellent person was counsel for him in his former petition to the consuls, that Varenus might be compelled to produce his accounts. Upon that occasion, as I attended Varenus merely as a friend, I determined to be silent. I thought it highly imprudent for me, who was appointed his counsel by the senate, to attempt to defend him as a person accused, when it was his business to insist that there was actually no charge subsisting against him. Accordingly, when Nigrinus had finished his speech, the consuls turning their eyes upon me, I rose up and said, *when they should hear what the real deputies from the province had to object against the motion of Nigrinus, they would be sensible that my silence was not without sufficient reason.* Upon this Nigrinus asked me to whom these deputies were sent? I replied, *That the decree of the province was directed to me among others.* He returned, *That is a point, tho' it may be clear to you, I am not so well*

¶ One of the Bithynians employed to manage the trial.

well satisfied of. To this I rejoined, *tho' it may not be so evident to you, who are concerned to support the accusation, it may be perfectly clear to me, who am on the more favourable side.* Then Polyænus the deputy from the province, acquainted the senate with the reasons for superseding the prosecution, but desired it might be without prejudice to Cæsar's determination. Magius answered him; Polyænus replied; as for himself, I only now and then threw in a word, observing in general, a profound silence. For I have learned, by experience, that upon some occasions there is as much rhetoric in silence, as in all the pomp of the most studied eloquence: and I remember, in some criminal cases, to have done even more service to my clients by a judicious taciturnity, than I could have expected from the most artful speech. To enter into the subject of eloquence, is indeed very foreign to the intent of my present letter, yet allow me to give you one instance in proof of the observation I just mentioned. A certain lady having lost her son, suspected that his freedmen, whom he had appointed coheirs with her, were guilty of forging the will and poisoning him. Accordingly, she charged them with the fact before the emperor, who directed Julianus Servianus to try the cause. I was counsel for the defendants, and the case being

ing exceedingly remarkable, and the advocates concerned on both fides of high reputation, it drew together a very numerous audience. The event was, the fervants being put to the torture, my clients were acquitted. But the mother applied a fecond time to the emperor, pretending fhe had difcovered fome new evidence. Servianus was therefore directed to rehear the caufe, that fhe might produce her frefh proofs. Julius Africanus was counfel for the mother: a young man of good parts, but little experience. He is grandfon to the famous orator of that name, of whom it is reported, that Paffienus Crifpus hearing him one day plead, archly-faid, *All this, I own, is very fine; but what is it to the purpofe?* Julius Africanus, I fay, having made a long harangue, and exhaufted the portion of time allotted to him, intreated Servianus to allow him to add one word more. When he had concluded, and the eyes of the whole affembly had been fixed a confiderable time upon me; *I would have anfwered Africanus,* I faid, *if he had given us that* one word *he beg'd leave to add, in which I doubt not he would have told us fomething we had not heard before.* I do not remember to have gained fo much applaufe by any fpeech I ever made, as I did in this inftance by making none. Thus the little that I

said

said for Varenus was received with the same general approbation. The consuls, agreeably to the request of Polyænus, reserved the whole affair for the determination of the emperor, whose resolution I impatiently wait for; as that will decide, whether I may be entirely at my ease with respect to Varenus; or must again renew all my trouble and solicitude upon his account. Farewel.

LETTER VII. *To* Saturninus.

THO' I had very lately made my acknowledgments to our friend Priscus, yet, since it was your desire, I willingly repeated them. It is with great pleasure I see so much harmony subsist between two such worthy men, whom I tenderly esteem, and that you consider each other's amity as a mutual obligation. For he professes also on his part to receive much happiness from yours, and, with a very generous contention, endeavours to rival you in that reciprocal affection, which time, I am persuaded, will augment.

I regret that any business should call you off from your studies. However, as soon as you shall have compromised (which you say you are upon the point of effecting) one of the causes you mention, and brought the other to a hearing, you will be at leisure

sure to enjoy the retirement of the country: and when you are satiated with repose, we may hope to see you in Rome. Farewel.

LETTER VIII. *To* Priscus.

THE frequent letters which I receive from Saturninus expressing his sense of your favours to him, afford me inexpressible satisfaction. May you go on as you began, and continue to cherish an affection for so worthy a man, from whose friendship you will receive a most sensible and lasting gratification. For, as he is greatly distinguished by every other virtue, so, particularly, by his invariable attachment to his friends. Farewel.

LETTER IX. *To* Tuscus.

YOU desire my sentiments concerning the method of study you should pursue, in that retirement to which you have long since withdrawn. In the first place then, I look upon it as a very advantageous practice (and it is what many recommend) to translate either from Greek into Latin, or from Latin into Greek. By this means you will furnish yourself not only with proper but brilliant expressions; with a variety of beautiful figures; and,

in

in short, acquire a nervous and powerful stile. Besides, by imitating the most approved authors, you will find your imagination insensibly catch their flame, and kindle into a similar warmth of invention; at the same time that those passages which you may possibly have overlooked in a common way of reading, cannot escape you in translating: and this method will also enlarge your knowledge, and improve your judgment. After you have read an eminent author, it may be proper, in order to make yourself more perfectly master of his subject and argument, to turn, from being his reader, to be his rival, as it were, and attempt something of your own upon the same topic; and then make an impartial comparison between your performance and his, in order to observe in what points either you or he have most happily succeeded. It will be a matter of very pleasing congratulation to yourself, if you should find in some articles, that you have the advantage of him, as it will be a great mortification if he should rise above you in all. You may sometimes venture in these little experimental essays, to try your strength upon the most shining passages of a distinguished author. The attempt, indeed, will be somewhat bold; but as it is a contention which passes in secret, it cannot be taxed with presumption. Not but that we have seen instances of persons, who have publicly entered this sort of lists with great success; and while they

did

did not despair of overtaking, have gloriously advanced before those whom they would have thought it sufficient honour to follow. After you have thus finished a composition, you may lay it aside, 'till it is no longer fresh in your memory, and then take it up, in order to revise and correct it. You will find several things to retain, but still more to reject; you will add a new thought here, and alter another there. It is a laborious and tedious task, I own, thus to re-enflame the mind after its first ardour has subsided; to recover an impulse when its force has been checked and spent; in a word, to interweave new parts into the texture of a composition, without disturbing or confounding the original plan; but the advantage attending this method will overbalance the difficulty. I know your present attention is principally directed towards the eloquence of the bar; but I would not for that reason advise you never to quit the polemic, if I may so call it, and contentious stile. As land is improved by sowing it with various seeds, so is the mind by exercising it with different studies. I would recommend it to you, therefore, sometimes to single out a fine passage of history; and sometimes to exercise yourself in the epistolary stile. For it frequently happens, that in pleading, one has occasion to introduce historical, and even poetical descriptions; as by studying the

epistolary

epistolary manner of writing, you will acquire a concise and easy expression. It will be extremely advantageous also to unbend your mind by poetical compositions: when I say so, I do not mean that species of poetry which turns upon subjects of great length (*such* being suitable only for persons of much leisure) but those little pieces of the sprightly kind of poesy, which serve as proper reliefs to, and are consistent with, employments of every sort. They commonly go under the title of *poetical amusements*; but these amusements have sometimes gained as much reputation to their authors, as works of a more serious nature; and thus (for while I am exhorting you to poetry, why should I not turn poet myself?)

> *As yielding wax the Artist's skill commands,*
> *Submissive shap'd beneath his forming hands;*
> *Now dreadful stands in arms a Mars confest;*
> *Or now with Venus' softer air imprest;*
> *A wanton Cupid now the mold belies;*
> *Now shines, severely chaste, a Pallas wise:*
> *As not alone to quench the raging flame,*
> *The sacred fountain pours her friendly stream;*
> *But sweetly gliding thro' the flow'ry green,*
> *Spreads glad refreshment o'er the smiling scene:*
> *So, form'd by science, should the ductile mind*
> *Receive, distinct, each various art refin'd.*

In

In this manner the greatest men, as well as the most eminent orators, accustomed either to exercise or amuse themselves, or rather indeed both. It is surprising how much the mind is entertained and refreshed by these little poetical compositions, as they turn upon subjects of gallantry, satire, tenderness, manners, and every thing, in short, that concerns life and the affairs of the world. Besides, the same advantage attends the exercising our minds in this inferiour species of poesy, as in every other sort; we turn from them to the easier composition of prose with so much the more pleasure, after having experienced the difficulty of being constrained and fettered by numbers.

And now, perhaps, I have enlarged upon the question you proposed to me more than you desired; nevertheless, there is still one article which I have omitted: I have not told you what kind of authors you should read; tho' indeed that was sufficiently implied when I mentioned the subjects I would recommend for your compositions. You will remember, that the most approved writers of each sort are to be carefully selected: for, as it has been well observed, " though we should read much, we " should not read many [a] books." Who those authors are, is so clearly settled, and so generally known,
that

[a] Thus the noble and polite moralist, speaking of the influence which our reading has upon our *taste* and *manners*, thinks it improper " to call a man *well-read*, who reads many " authors;

that I need not particularly name them; besides, I have already extended this letter to such an immoderate length, that I fear I have too long interrupted those studies, the method of which I have been pointing out to you. I will here resign you therefore to your tablets, either to resume the studies in which you were before engaged, or to enter upon some of those I have recommended. Farewel.

"authors; since he must of necessity have more ill models than good: and be more stuffed with bombast, ill fancy, and wry thought, than filled with solid sense and just imagination." [Charact. v. 1. 142.] When the Goths over-ran Greece, the libraries escaped their destruction by a notion which some of their leaders industriously propagated among them, that it would be more for their interest to leave those spoils untouched to their enemies; as being proper to enervate their minds, and amuse them with vain and idle speculations. Truth perhaps has been less a gainer by this multiplicity of books, than error; and it may be a question, whether the excellent models which have been delivered down to us from antiquity, together with those few which modern times have produced, by any means balance the immoderate weight which must be thrown into the opposite scale of writers. The truth is, tho' we may be learned by other men's reflections, wise we can only be by our own: and the maxim here recommended by Pliny, would well deserve the attention of the studious, though no other inconvenience attended the reading of many books, than that which Sir William Temple apprehends from it; the lessening the force and growth of a man's own genius. For it may be justly doubted, with that ingenious author, "whether the weight and number of so many other men's thoughts and notions, may not suppress his own, or hinder the motion or agitation of them, from which all invention arises; as heaping on wood, or too many sticks, or too close together, suppresses, and sometimes quite extinguishes a little spark, that would otherwise have grown up to a noble flame." [Essay on learning, v. 1. 158. fol. ed.]

LETTER X. To MACRINUS.

AS I always desire to know the end of an interesting story when it broke off before the conclusion; so, I imagine, you will be glad to be informed of the remaining part of the cause which I mentioned to you, [a] between the Bithynians and Varenus. It was pleaded before the emperor by Polyænus on one side, and Magius on the other. When Cæsar had heard both parties, *Neither party*, said he, *shall have reason to complain of delay; for I will take care to inform myself of the real sentiments of the province.* In the mean while, Varenus has gained a very considerable point; for can any circumstance make the justness of his accusation appear more doubtful, than that it is a question whether he is accused at all? We have only to wish, that the province may not again approve of the measure which, it is said, she now condemns, and repent of her former repentance. Farewel.

[a] See Let. VI. p. 8. of this B.

LETTER XI. *To* FABATUS[a].

YOU are surprized, I find, that my share of five-twelfths of the estate which lately fell to me, and which I had directed to be sold to the best bidder, should have been disposed of by my freed-man Hermes to Corellia (without putting it up to auction) at the rate of seven hundred thousand [b] sesterces for the whole. You think it might have produced nine hundred thousand [c]; and are so much the more desirous to know, whether I am inclined to ratify what he has done. I am; and for such reasons, I hope, as not only you will approve, but which will also excuse me to my joint-coheirs for having, upon a motive of superior obligation, separated my interest from theirs. I have the highest esteem for Corellia, both as the sister of Rufus, whose memory will ever be sacred to me, and as she was an intimate friend of my mother. Besides, that excellent man Minutius Tuscus, her husband, has every claim to my affection that a long friendship can give him; as there was likewise so strict an intimacy between her son and me, that I

fixed

---
[a] His wife's grandfather.
[b] About 5,600 l. of our money.
[c] About 7,200 l. of our money.

fixed upon him to preside at the games which I exhibited when I was elected Prætor. This lady, when I was last in the country, expressed a strong inclination to purchase some spot upon our lake of Comum; I therefore made her an offer, at her own price, of any quantity of my land there, except what came to me from my father and mother: for I could not consent to sell any part of my patrimonial estate, even to Corellia. When the inheritance in question fell to me, I wrote to acquaint her it was to be sold. This letter I sent by Hermes, who, upon her requesting him immediately to assign to her my proportion, consented. You see, therefore, how strongly my honour is engaged to confirm an act which my freed-man did, in pursuance of what he knew to be my inclinations. I have only to entreat my fellow-coheirs not to be offended that I have made a separate sale of what I had certainly a right to dispose of. They are under no necessity of being governed by my example, since they have not the same connections with Corellia; and are at full liberty therefore to be guided by interest, which in my own case I chose to sacrifice to friendship. Farewel.

LETTER XII. *To* MINUTIUS.

I Have delayed so much the longer sending you the petition which I have drawn up for the use of your, or rather I should say *our* friend, (for what is there we do not possess in common?) that you might not have time to correct it, that is, to render all the pains I have taken, ineffectual. After all, whether you may or may not find time for that purpose, I know not; but of this I am sure, you will most certainly spoil it, if, agreeably to the very *delicate* taste of your very *refined* critics, you should throw out its most shining parts. I shall forgive you, however, if you should, and shall upon some future occasion, successfully make use of what your fastidious niceness rejects; as in some future composition I doubt not to receive much applause for those different expressions which I have interlined. I suspected you would call every thing unnatural and bombast which is raised above the style of ordinary language; I thought proper therefore for your ease, to vary the phrase, and take it somewhat lower, or rather indeed, to debase it; tho' you, I know (for I must continue to rally your *nice* taste) will esteem it an improvement. Thus far, in order to make you smile in the midst of your serious occupations, I have indulged a jocose humour; but
without

without doubt, I am wond'rous *serious* when I add, that I expect to be reimbursed my charges in sending a courier express with this petition. Now are you not disposed to condemn it, not only in some of it's parts, but in the whole, and insist, that you ought not pay for a *thing* which is absolutely of no *value?* Farewel.

LETTER XIII. *To* Ferox.

I Find by your letter, that you do, and do not study. This will appear a little enigmatical till I explain it: you expressly say, indeed, that you have bidden adieu to study; but such a vein of elegance runs through your whole letter, that it is impossible it should have been composed without much thought; unless you are privileged beyond the rest of mankind, and can express such admirable sentiments in so polished a style, carelessly and with a flowing pen. Farewel.

LETTER XIV. *To* Corellia.

YOU are truly generous to desire and insist, that I take for my share of the estate you purchased of me, not after the rate of seven hundred thousand sesterces [a] for the whole, as my freed-

---

[a] See letter the 11th of this book.

freed-man fold it to you; but in the proportion of nine hundred thousand, agreeable to what you gave to the farmers of the [b] twentieths for their part. But I must desire and insist in my turn, that you consider not only what is suitable to your character, but what is worthy of mine; and that you suffer me to oppose your inclination in this single instance, with the same warmth that I obey it in all others. Farewel.

LETTER XV. *To* Saturninus.

YOU ask me *how I spend my time?* You know how much of it is disposed in the business of my post; what remains I devote to the service of my friends, and sometimes to my books: and altho' I will not venture to affirm it would be better, I am sure it would be happier, if I could say that the latter, not only *sometimes,* but constantly engages me. I should be concerned to hear, that your occupations are of the sort least agreeable to your inclinations, if I did not know that

---

[b] Augustus imposed a tax of the 20th part of all legacies and inheritances, which he appropriated to the support of the army. This was deemed a heavy imposition, and accordingly it was eased in several points by succeeding emperors, particularly by Trajan, as appears from our author's noble panegyric upon him [Sect 37, &c.] but it was not wholly abolished till the time of Antoninus Pius.

that to be active in the affairs of one's native corporation, and in settling controversies among one's friends there, are employments of the most laudable kind.

I was well persuaded the company of our friend Priscus would be extremely agreeable to you, sensible as I am of the amiable simplicity and politeness of his manners; but I had yet to learn (what I had the pleasure to be informed by your letter) that he is also the most grateful of men, by so kindly remembering the little services I have done him. Farewel.

LETTER XVI. *To* FABATUS.

CALESTRIUS TIRO, to whom I am united by every public and private connection, is in the number of my most intimate friends. We served together in the army, and were both of us [a] Quæstors at the same time to Cæsar. He got the start of me indeed, in the Tribunate, by the privilege which the law gives to those who have [b] children; but

---

[a] An office resembling that of our secretary of state.

[b] A law at first proposed by Augustus, but which afterwards with several alterations passed in the consulship of Papius and Poppeas, A. U. 762; in which, amongst other things, it was enacted, " That all magistrates should take precedence according to the number of their children; that in elections those candidates should be preferred who had the most numerous offspring: and that any person might stand sooner than ordinary for an office, if he had as many children as he wanted years to be legally capable of such a dignity." Vid. Lipsii Excurs. ad. Tacit. An. 1. 3.

but I overtook him in the Prætorship by the indulgence of the emperor, who dispensed with my wanting a year of the legal age for that office. I frequently retire with him to his country villas, and he often takes the benefit of change of air at mine. He is lately appointed proconsul of Bœtica, and proposes to pass thro' ᶜ Ticinum, in his way to that province. I hope, and indeed am well assured, I can easily prevail with him to turn out of his road to your house, if you should have an inclination to make any of those slaves free before a magistrate, to whom you have already given their liberty ᵈ in the presence of your friends. You need be under no apprehension that he will look upon this as a trouble, as I am sure he would willingly travel round the world for my sake. I beg you therefore to lay aside all scruple, and only consider what will be most agreeable to yourself; for, be assured, he will take as much pleasure in executing my requests, as I do in obeying yours. Farewel.

ᶜ Pavia in the dutchy of Milan.
ᵈ This last method only discharged them from servitude, but did not entitle them to the privileges of complete freedom.

LETTER XVII. *To* CELER.

Every author has his particular reasons for reciting his works; mine, I have often said, is in order, if any error should have escaped my own observation, (as no doubt is probable) to have it pointed out to me. I cannot therefore but be surprized to find (what your letter assures me), that there are some who blame me for reciting my speeches; unless, perhaps, they are of opinion, that *this* is the single species of composition which ought to be privileged from correction. If so, I would willingly ask them why they allow (if perchance they vouchsafe to allow) that History may be recited, since it is a work which ought to be devoted to truth, not ostentation? or why Tragedy, as it is composed for action and the stage, not for being read to a private audience? or Lyric Poetry, as it is not a reader, but a chorus of voices and instruments that it requires? They will reply, perhaps, that in the instances mentioned, custom has made the practice in question usual: I should be glad to know then, if they think the person who first introduced this practice is to be condemned? Besides, the rehearsal of orations is no unprecedented thing either with us or the Grecians. Still, perhaps, they will insist, that it can answer no purpose to recite a speech which has previously been

been delivered in public. There would be some force in this objection, if one were immediately to repeat the very same performance, and to the very same audience; but if you make several additions and alterations; if your audience is composed partly of the same, and partly of different persons, and the recital is at some distance of time; why is there less propriety in rehearsing your speech than in publishing it? "But it is difficult," say the objectors, "to give satisfaction to an audience by "the mere reading of a speech:" *that* is a reason which concerns the particular skill and pains of the person who rehearses, but by no means holds against recitation in general. In fact, it is not while I am reading, but when I am read, that I aim at approbation; and upon this principle it is, that I omit no sort of method which may render my performances more correct. Accordingly, I again and again revise my compositions in private; afterwards read them to two or three friends; and then give them to a few others to make their remarks. If I have still any doubt concerning the justness of their observations, I carefully reconsider them with another friend or two; and then finally recite them to a more numerous assembly. This is the time, believe me, when I find myself best qualified to exercise all the severity of criticism; for my attention rises in proportion to

my

my solicitude; as nothing renders the judgement so acute to discern errors as that modest respect and reverence one feels for one's audience upon those occasions. For tell me, whether you would not be infinitely less affected if you were to speak before a single person only, tho' ever so learned, than before a numerous assembly, even tho' it were composed of none but illiterate people? When you rise up to plead, are you not at that juncture, above all others, most diffident of your powers? and do you not wish, I will not say some particular parts only, but that the whole frame of your intended speech were altered? especially if the circle should be large in which you are to speak; for, there is something in a crowded audience, even of the most vulgar kind, that strikes one with awe. And if you suspect at the first opening of your speech that you are not well received, do you not find all the energy of your mind weakened, and the whole strength of your abilities sink under you? The reason I imagine to be, that there is I know not what dignity in the collective sentiments of a multitude; and tho' separately their judgement is, perhaps, of little weight, yet when united it becomes respectable. Agreeably to this notion, Pomponius Secundus, the famous tragic poet, whenever his friends and he differed about the retaining or rejecting any passage in

his

his dramatic writings, used to say *I appeal* [a] *to the people*; and accordingly by their silence or applause, adopted either his own or his friends' sentiments: such was the regard he paid to the populace! [b] Whether with justice or not, does not concern me to determine, as I never recite my works publicly, but only before a select number of friends, whose presence I respect, and whose judgement I value; in

[a] There is a kind of witticism in this expression, which will be lost to the mere English reader, unless he be informed that the Romans had a privilege, confirmed to them by several laws which passed in the earlier ages of the republic, of appealing from the decisions of the magistrates, to the general assembly of the people: and the form of appeal was in the same words which Pomponius here applies to a different purpose.

[b] However unsafe in general, an appeal to the vulgar notions may be, there are yet some cases in which their sentiments have ever been received by the judicious, as decisive. The merit of performances in the persuasive, or imitative arts, so far as the mere raising or representing the passions are concerned, will best be tried by the effect they produce on plain and untutored minds: for (as Tully observes) " that artist who has nature for his object, must certainly " fall short of the truth of his art, where nature is not " moved *." The custom which prevailed among the Romans of reciting their works of genius in the porticos and places of public resort, took its rise probably from the same notion of a general and innate taste being implanted in all mankind of what is just and natural in the moving arts. It was upon this principle likewise that the great masters in painting and statuary in ancient Greece, exhibited their performances to public view, and corrected them by the popular feelings. There is a remarkable story of Annibal Carrachi, which shews he appealed to the same standard. He observed that a famous picture of Domenichino's, representing the flagellation of St. Andrew, made a very strong impression upon an old woman, who, at the same time

* De orat. lib. 1.

in a word, whose opinions I observe as if they were so many individuals I had separately consulted; at the same time that I stand in as much awe before them as I should before the most numerous assembly. What Cicero says of the *pen*, will, in my opinion, hold equally true of that dread we have of the public: " It is the most rigid critic imagin-" able [a]." The very fear of reciting; of entering an assembly; and the reverential concern when one appears there; each of these circumstances being impressed upon the composer's mind, tend to improve and perfect his performance. Upon the whole therefore, I cannot repent of a practice which I have experienced to be so exceedingly beneficial; and far from being discouraged by the trifling objections of these censors, I request you to point out to me, if there be any other method of correction, that I may also adopt it; for nothing can sufficiently satisfy my anxiety to render my compositions perfect. I reflect what an arduous

time seemed little affected with another picture of a martyrdom done by Guido, which was placed near it. A debate afterwards happening about the respective merit of these two performances, Carrachi decided the dispute by only relating this fact [*]. Thus, as the poet observes,

——*The people's voice is odd,*
It is, and it is not, the voice of God. POPE.

[a] *Stilus est optimus & præstantissimus dicendi effector atque magister.* De Orat. l. 33.

[*] The well-known appeal of Moliere to his old house-keeper, cannot but occur to the reader as a remarkable instance of the same kind.

duous adventure it is to resign any work into the hands of the public; and I cannot but be persuaded, that frequent revisals and many consultations, must go to the finishing of a performance, which one desires should universally, and for ever please. Farewel.

LETTER XVIII. *To* CANINIUS.

YOU ask my advice in what manner you shall settle the sum of money, which you have presented to our fellow-citizens of Comum for an annual festival, so as to secure the just application of it after your death. Your question proceeds from a truly generous principle; but the answer is not very easy. If you pay down the money to the community; there is great danger that it will be squandered away. If you settle lands for that purpose; they will probably be ill cultivated, as those of the public usually are. Upon the whole then, I can think of no method more eligible than what I pursued myself in a parallel instance. Intending to give * five hundred thousand sesterces for the maintenance of children who were born of good families, I made a fictitious sale to the public agent, of an estate in land which was worth considerably more, who reconveyed it back to me, charged

* About 4,000 l. of our money.

charged with a yearly rent of [b] 30,000 sesterces. By these means the principal was secured to the community, at the same time that the interest was certain, and the estate itself (as it was of much greater value than the rent charged upon it) was always sure of finding a tenant. I am well aware, indeed, that by this method I have actually given more than I appear to have done, as the value of the whole estate will be much lessened by the incumbrance with which it is charged. But the interest of the public ought always to supercede every private consideration, as what is eternal is to be preferred to what is mortal; and a man of true generosity will study in what manner to render his benefaction most advantageous, rather than how he may bestow it with least expence. Farewel.

LETTER XIX. *To* Priscus.

I AM deeply afflicted by the ill state of health of my friend Fannia, which she contracted during her attendance on Junia, one of the Vestal virgins. She

---

[b] About 240 l. of our money. It should seem by this passage, that the rate of interest of money upon mortgage among the Romans in Pliny's time, or rather at the time when he wrote this letter (for no doubt it varied with public circumstances) was at 6 *per Cent.* as in the common way of loan, upon personal security. It appears from the sixty-second letter of the tenth book, to have been so high as 12 *per Cent.*

She engaged in this good office at first voluntarily, Junia being her relation; but was afterwards appointed to it by an order from the college of Priests: for, these virgins, when any indisposition makes it necessary to remove them from the temple of Vesta, are always delivered into the care and custody of some venerable matron. It was her assiduity in the execution of this charge that occasioned her present disorder, which is a continual fever, attended with a cough that increases daily. She is extremely emaciated, and every part of her frame seems in a total decay except her spirits; those indeed she preserves in their full vigour, and with a fortitude worthy the wife of Helvidius, and the daughter of Thrasea. In every other article, her health is so greatly impaired, that I am more than apprehensive upon her account; I am deeply afflicted. I grieve, my friend, that so excellent a woman is going to be removed from the world, which will never, perhaps, again behold her equal. How eminent is her chastity, her piety, her gravity, her courage! She twice followed her husband into exile, and once was banished herself upon his account. For, Senecio, when he was arraigned for writing the life of Helvidius, having said in his defence that he composed that work at the request of Fannia; Metius Carus, with a stern and threatening air, asked her whether

ther it was true? She acknowledged it was: and when he farther queſtioned her, whether ſhe ſupplied him likewiſe with materials for that purpoſe, and whether her mother was privy to this tranſaction? ſhe boldly confeſſed the former, but abſolutely denied the latter. In ſhort, throughout her whole examination, not a word eſcaped her which betrayed the leaſt timidity. On the contrary, ſhe had the courage to preſerve a copy of thoſe very books which the ſenate, over-awed by the tyranny of the times, had ordered to be ſuppreſſed, and the effects of the author to be confiſcated; taking with her as her companions, thoſe obnoxious volumes which had been the cauſe of her exile. How pleaſing is her converſation, how polite her addreſs, and (which ſeldom unites in the ſame character) how venerable her whole demeanour! She will hereafter, I am well perſuaded, be pointed out as a model to all wives; and perhaps be deemed worthy to be held forth as an example of fortitude even to our ſex: I am ſure, at leaſt, that we who have the pleaſure of ſeeing and converſing with her, contem--plate her with the ſame admiration, as thoſe female heroines who are celebrated in ancient ſtory. I confeſs, I cannot but tremble for this illuſtrious houſe as it ſeems ſhaken to its very foundation,

tion, and falling into ruin with this excellent woman: for, though she will leave descendants behind her, yet what a height of virtue must they attain, what glorious actions must they perform, ere the world will be persuaded that she was not the last of her family! It is an aggravating circumstance of affliction to me, that by her death, I seem to lose a second time her mother; that worthy mother (and what can I say higher in her praise) of so amiable a woman! who, as she was restored to me in her daughter, so she will now again be taken from me, and the loss of Fannia will thus pierce my heart at once with a fresh stab, and tear open a former wound. I so truly loved and honoured them both, that I know not which had the greatest share of my affection and esteem: and it was a question they wished might ever remain undetermined. In their prosperity and their adversity I performed every good office to them in my power; and was their comforter in exile, as well as their avenger at their return. But I have not yet discharged all the obligations I owe them; and am so much the more solicitous for the recovery of this lady, that I may have time to acquit the full claim she has upon my kindest offices. Such is the anxiety under which I write this letter! But if some friendly power should happily give me

occasion

occasion to exchange it for sentiments of joy, I shall not complain of the alarms I now suffer. Farewel.

LETTER XX. *To* TACITUS.

I Have perused your book with all the attention I was master of, and have marked the passages I think should be altered, and those which I am of opinion ought intirely to be thrown out. It is as habitual to me to speak truth, as it is agreeable to you to hear it; and indeed none are more patient of censure, than those who have the best claim to applause. I now expect, in return, your observations upon that treatise of mine which I lately sent you. How agreeable, how noble is such a commerce! and how am I pleased with the thought, that posterity, if it shall at all concern itself with us, will not cease to mention with what harmony, what freedom, what fidelity we lived together! It will be an instance as remarkable, as it is uncommon, that two persons nearly of the same age and rank, and of some character in the republic of letters (for since I join myself with you, I am obliged to speak of your merit with reserve) should thus mutually assist and promote each other's studies. When I was a very young man, and you in the prime of your glory and reputation, I endeavoured to follow your steps,

steps, and was desirous to be considered as next in fame to you,

*But next with many a length between!*ᵃ

And tho' there were, at that time, many celebrated geniuses in Rome, yet you, of all others, appeared to me, not only most worthy to be my model, but from a similitude of our dispositions, most easy for me to copy. It is particularly agreeable to me therefore to find, that in all companies where literature is the topic of conversation, we are always mentioned together, and that my name immediately follows yours. It is true, there are some who prefer you to me, as others, on the contrary, give me the advantage; but I am little solicitous in what order we are placed, so that we stand together; for, in my estimation, whoever is next to you must necessarily precede every one else. You even see in ᵇ wills (unless

---

ᵃ Virg. Æn. Pitt's Transl.
ᵇ " It was the peculiar custom of Rome, for the clients and
" dependents of families, to bequeath at their death to their
" patrons some considerable part of their estates, as the most
" effectual testimony of their respect and gratitude; and the
" more a man received in this way, the more it redounded to
" his credit. Thus Cicero mentions it to the honour of Lu-
" cullus, that, while he governed Asia as Proconsul, many
" great estates were left to him by will. And Nepos tells us,
" in praise of Atticus, that he succeeded to many inheritances
" of the same kind, bequeathed to him on no other account
" than of his friendly and amiable temper. Cicero, when he
" was

less in the case of particular friendship to either of us) we are always equally considered, and that the legacies bequeathed to us are generally the same, both in number and value. Since therefore, we are thus united by a similitude of studies, manners, reputation, and even by testamentary donations, those last instances of the world's good opinion; should not these circumstances tend to enflame us mutually with the most ardent affection? Farewel.

LETTER XXI. *To* Cornutus.

I Obey, my dearest Collegue, your commands to favour the weakness of my eyes; and accordingly I came hither in a covered litter, in which I was as much sheltered as if I had been in my chamber. I forbear too (with reluctance indeed, however I do forbear) both writing and reading; and it is with my ears only that I study. By drawing the curtains of my chamber, I make it gloomy, but not dark; and when I walk in my covered portico, I shut the lower range of windows, and by that means enjoy as much shade as light. Thus I endeavour to accustom myself to the light by degrees.

" was falsely reproached by Antony, with being neglected on
" these occasions, declared in his reply, that he had gained
" from this single article, about two hundred thousand
" pounds," Middleton's Life of Tully, v. 2. 514.

degrees. The bath being of service in this case, I allow myself the use of it; as also of wine, because it is not judged prejudicial, but I drink it with great moderation. I do so, you know, at all times, but particularly now that I have * one who narrowly observes me.—I received the pullet, with great pleasure as coming from you; and weak as my eyes still are, they are strong enough, however, to discern it is extremely fat. Farewel.

LETTER XXII. *To* FALCO.

YOU will not wonder I so earnestly pressed you to confer the Tribunate upon my friend, when you shall be informed who and what he is; and as you have complied with my request, I may now acquaint you with his name and character. It is Cornelius Minutianus, who both in rank and merit is the ornament of that province to which I owe my birth. His family and fortune are noble, and yet he cultivates science with as much application, as if the narrowness of his circumstances rendered it necessary. He is a most upright judge, a most strenuous advocate, a most faithful friend. You will look upon the obligation as done to yourself, when you shall have an opportunity of becoming

---

* Meaning his wife, perhaps, or his physician.

ing better acquainted with this excellent person, who (not to speak in too lofty terms of so modest a man) is equal to all the honours and titles that can be conferred upon him. Farewel.

LETTER XXIII. *To* FABATUS[a].

I Greatly rejoice that you have so much recovered your strength as to be able to take so long a journey as to [b] Mediolanum, in order to meet Tiro; but, that you may continue to enjoy that happiness, let me intreat you to spare yourself a fatigue so improper for a man of your years. I must even insist, that you wait for him at Comum, and that you do not stir out of your own house, nor even out of your chamber, to receive him. As I love him with the affection of a brother, it would be unreasonable he should expect from the person whom I honour as my parent, a point of ceremony which he would spare his own. Farewel.

[a] His wife's grandfather.
[b] Milan.

LETTER XXIV. *To* Geminius.

Numidia Quadratilla is lately dead, having lived almost to her eightieth year. She enjoyed, 'till her last sickness, an uninterrupted state of health, with a strength and firmness of body unusual to persons of her sex. She has left a very prudent will, having disposed of two thirds of her estate to her grand-son, and the rest to her grand-daughter. With the young lady I have little acquaintance, but the grand-son is one of the most favourite and intimate friends I have. He is a person of singular worth; and his merit entitles him to the affection of a relation, even where his blood does not. Tho' he is extremely beautiful, he escaped every malicious imputation both whilst a boy and when a youth: he was a husband at four and twenty, and would have been a father if providence had not disappointed his hopes. Notwithstanding he resided in the family with his grand-mother, who was exceedingly devoted to the pleasures of the town, yet he observed great severity of conduct himself, at the same time that he behaved to her with the utmost respect. She retained a set of * Pantomimes,

---

* These Pantomimes were, as their name imports, universal mimics, whose humour consisted in imitating the peculiar manner

tomimes, and was an encourager of this sort of people, to a degree inconsistent with a person of her sex and rank. But Quadratus never appeared at these entertainments, not only when she exhibited them in the theatre, but even in her own house; nor indeed did she require him to be present. I once heard her say, when she was recommending the studies of her grand-son to my inspection, that it was her custom, in order to pass away some of those unemployed hours with which female life abounds, to amuse herself with playing at ᵇ chess, or seeing the

---

ner and gesture of particular persons. They were at first introduced upon the stage, as Scaliger supposes, to succeed the chorus and comedies, and divert the audience with buffoon postures and antic dances. In after times those interludes became distinct entertainments, and were exhibited apart from other plays. But the use of these Pantomimes was not confined to the stage only, for Suetonius informs us, they were introduced in funeral solemnities, in order to represent the manner of the deceased.

ᵇ This game among the Romans seems to have been much of the same nature, though by Quadratilla dismissing her grand-son when she played at it, not in the same estimation as a *female* amusement, with modern chess. Their men, which they called *Calculi* or *Latrunculi*, were made sometimes of wax, and sometimes of glass, and were distinguished by black and white colours. The invention of it has been carried by some so high as the siege of Troy, but Peter Texeiras in his history of Persia (as quoted by Pitiscus in his Lex. Antiq. Rom.) imagines it to be of Persian original, because, says he, in all countries where this game is played, the names of the men are either the same with, or plainly a corruption of those given to them in the Persian language. Allusions to this game are frequent in the classic writers; but the fullest description of it is contained in the following lines, taken from the little poem address'd to Piso, which is

to

the mimicry of her pantomimes; but that whenever she engaged in either of those amusements, she constantly dismissed her grand-son to his studies: a dismission to be found at the end of some editions of Lucan, and is generally ascribed to that author:

Te si forte juvat, studiorum pondere fessum,
Non languere tamen, lususque movere per artem,
Callidiore modo Tabula variatur aperta
Calculus, et vitreo peraguntur milite bella,
Ut niveus nigros, nunc et niger alliget albos.
Sed tibi quis non terga dedit? quis te duce cessit
Calculus? aut quis non periturus perdidit hostem?
Mille modis acies tua dimicat: ille petentem
Dum fugit, ipse rapit: longo venit ille recessu
Qui stetit in speculis: hic se committere rixæ
Audet, et in prædam venientem decipit hostem:
Ancipites subit ille moras, similisque ligato
Obligat ipse duos: hic ad majora movetur,
Ut citus et fracta prorumpat in agmina mandra,
Clausaque dejecto populatur mœnia vallo.
Interea, sectis quamvis accerima surgunt
Prælia militibus, plena tamen ipse phalange,
Aut etiam pauco spoliata milite vincis,
Et tibi captivæ resonat manus utraque turbæ.

Ad Pison. Poëmation.

When, to relieve the labours of thy mind,
Thou turn'st from deep research in arts refin'd,
Not in soft indolence you waste the hour,
But happier genius still exerts its pow'r;
To mimic war the radiant troops are led,
And martial ranks the varied table spread;
There sable bands, and *here* a snow-white train,
With doubtful fate of war the fight maintain.
But who with thee shall dare dispute the field?
Led by thy hand, what warrior knows to yield?
Or if he fall, he falls with glorious pride,
His vanquish'd foe extended by his side.
Unnumber'd stratagems thy forces try;
Now artful feign, and only feign, to fly,

Now

a dismission which proceeded, I am inclined to think, as much out of a certain reverential awe she felt upon those occasions in the presence of the youth, as from her affection towards him. I was a good deal surprized, as I believe you will be, at what he told me the last time the Pontifical [c] games were exhibited. As we were coming out of the theatre together, where we had been entertained with her pantomimes, *Do you know,* said he, *this is the first time I ever saw Quadratilla's freedman dance?* Such was the striking declaration her grand-son made! while a set of men of a far different character, in order to do honour to Quadratilla (I am ashamed to call it *honour*) with the lowest and grossest flattery were running up and down the theatre,
affecting

<pre>
Now boldly rushes 'midst the ranks of war,
The chief who view'd the slaught'ring scene from far.
This, bravely daring in the arduous toil,
Repels the host advancing to the spoil,
While cautious *that* moves dreadful on and slow,
And fraudful meditates the certain blow;
What tho' in guise a slave he seems in chains,
Two captives He in durance close detains.
But see, yon hero with impetuous haste,
Bursts thro' the ranks, and lays the ramparts waste!
While thus the mighty battle glows around,
And prostrate chiefs bestrow the well-fought ground,
Full and unbroken lo! thy squadrons stand,
Or scarce one warrior lost of thy command;
The captive crowds thy victory proclaim,
And foes confess thy undisputed fame.
</pre>

[c] The priests, as well as other magistrates, exhibited public games to the people when they entered upon their office. It should seem by what follows, that *Quadratilla* had lent her troop of Pantomimes to honour the celebration of these Pontifical games.

affecting the utmoſt admiration and rapture at the performances of theſe her pantomimes, and then imitating, in muſical chant, the *mein and manner* of their lady patroneſs. But now all that theſe theatrical flatterers have obtained in return, is only a few trifling legacies, which they have the mortification to receive from an heir, who never but once deigned to be preſent at Quadratilla's ſhews.—I ſend you this account, as knowing you are not diſpleaſed to hear the news of the town, and becauſe, when any occurrence has rejoiced me, I love to renew it again, by communicating it to my friends. And indeed the laudable affection which Quadratilla has ſhewn in her will to her two heirs, and the particular honour done therein to that excellent youth her grand-ſon, has afforded me a very ſenſible ſatisfaction; as I am extremely glad too, that the houſe which once belonged to Caſſius, the founder and chief of the ᵈ Caſſian ſchool, is come into the poſſeſſion of a perſon not leſs reſpectable than its former maſter. For, my worthy friend will fill it as he ought, and its ancient luſtre will again revive under Quadratus; who, I am perſuaded, will prove as eminent an orator, as Caſſius was a lawyer. Farewel.

ᵈ A famous lawyer who flouriſhed in the reign of the emperor Claudius: thoſe who followed his juridical opinions, were ſaid to be Caſſiani, or of the ſchool of Caſſius.

LETTER XXV. *To* Rufus.

WHAT numbers of learned men does modesty conceal, or love of retirement withdraw, from public fame! and yet when we are going to speak or recite in numerous assemblies, it is the judgement only of popular and ostentatious talents of which we stand in awe; whereas we have more reason to revere the decisions of those who cultivate the sciences in contemplative life, and form their opinions of works of genius in privacy and silence, undistracted by the noise of clamorous assemblies: an observation which I give you upon experience. Terentius Junior having passed thro' the military offices suitable to a person of Equestrian rank, and executed with great integrity the post of receiver-general of the revenues in [a] Narbonensian Gaul, retired to his estate; preferring the enjoyment of an uninterrupted tranquillity, to those honours which his services had merited. He invited me lately to his house, where, looking upon him only as a worthy master of a family, and an industrious farmer, I started such rural topics of conversation, in which I imagined he was most versed. But he soon turned the discourse, and displaying a great fund of

---

[a] One of the four principal divisions of ancient Gaul: it extended from the Pyrenæan mountains, which separate France from Spain, to the Alps, which divide it from Italy, and comprehended Languedoc, Provence, Dauphiny, and Savoy.

of knowledge, entered upon subjects of literature. I was astonished at the elegance with which he expressed himself both in Latin and Greek! for he is so perfectly well skilled in each, that which ever he speaks, seems to be the language wherein he particularly excels. How extensive is his reading! how tenacious his memory! You would not imagine him the inhabitant of an ignorant country village, but a citizen of the learned Athens. In short, his conversation has increased my solicitude concerning my works, and taught me to revere the judgement of these studious country gentlemen, as much as that of more known and distinguished literati. Let me persuade you to consider them in the same light; for believe me, upon a careful observation, you will often find in the literary as well as military world, most powerful abilities concealed under a rustic garb. Farewel.

LETTER XXVI. *To* Maximus.

THE lingering disorder of a friend of mine gave me occasion lately to reflect, that we are always in the best moral disposition when afflicted with sickness. Where is the man, who, labouring under the pain of any distemper, is either solicited by avarice or enflamed with lust? At such a season he is neither the slave of love, nor the fool of ambition; he looks with indifference

ference upon the charms of wealth, and is contented with ever so small a portion of it, as being upon the point of leaving even that little. It is *then* he recollects there are Gods, and that he himself is but a [a] man: no mortal is *then* the object of his envy, his admiration, or his contempt; and having no malice to gratify, the tales of slander excite not his attention: his dreams run only upon the refreshment of [b] baths and fountains. These are the supreme objects of his thoughts and wishes, while he resolves, if he should recover, to pass the remainder of his days disengaged from the cares and business of the world; that is, in innocence and happiness. I may therefore lay down to you and myself a short rule, which the philosophers have endeavoured to inculcate at the expence of many words, and even many volumes; that "we should realize in health, those resolutions we form in sickness." Farewel.

[a] The awakening power of adversity in general, is so beautifully described by the banished duke in Shakespeare's *As you like it*, that it will not, perhaps, be deemed foreign to the purpose to produce it as a parallel passage, especially as the sentiment in the second line is exactly the same with this of Pliny's before us:

This is no flattery: These are counsellors
That *feelingly persuade me what I am.*
Sweet are the uses of adversity,
Which like the toad, ugly and venomous,
Wears yet a precious jewel in his head. Act. 2. Sc. 1.

[b] The ancient physicians advised bathing as of sovereign efficacy in various disorders.

LETTER XXVII. *To* Sura.

THE present recess from business affords you leisure to communicate, and me to receive, information. I am very desirous to know your opinion concerning spectres; whether you believe they have a real existence, and are a sort of divinities, or are only the visionary impressions of a terrified imagination? What particularly inclines me to give credit to their reality, is a story[a] which I lately heard of Curtius Rufus. When he was in low circumstances, and unknown in the world, he attended the governour of Africa into that province. One evening as he was walking in the public portico, he was extremely surprized with the apparition of a woman, whose figure and beauty were more than human. She told him she was the tutelar power who presided over Africa, and was come to inform him of the future events of his life: that he should go back to Rome, where he should be raised to the highest honours; should return to that province invested with the proconsular dignity, and there should die. Accordingly every circumstance of this prediction was actually accom-

---

[a] This story is likewise related by Tacitus in the 11th book of his annals, chap. 21.

accomplished. It is said farther, that upon his arrival at Carthage, as he was coming out of the ship, the same figure accosted him upon the shore. It is certain, at least, that being seized with a fit of illness, tho' there were no symptoms in his case that led his attendants to despair, he instantly gave up all hope of recovery; judging, it should seem, of the truth of the future part of the prophecy, by that which had already been fulfilled, and of the misfortune which threatened him, by the success which he had experienced. To this story let me add another not less remarkable than the former, but attended with more terrifying circumstances: and I will give it you exactly as it was related to me. There was at Athens [b] a large and commodious house, which lay under the disrepute of being haunted. In the dead of the night a noise, resembling the clashing of iron, was frequently heard, which, if you listened more attentively, sounded like the rattling of chains. At first it seemed distant, but approached nearer by degrees, till a spectre appeared in the form of an old man, extremely meagre and ghastly, with a long beard and dishevelled hair, rattling the chains on his feet and hands. The distressed inhabitants in the

---

[b] Lucian ridicules a story pretty much resembling this, but lays the scene of it in Corinth. Vid. Lucian. Philopseud.

mean while paſſed their nights under the moſt dreadful terrors imaginable. This, as it broke their reſt, ruined alſo their health, and brought on diſtempers, which, together with their conſtant horrors of mind, proved in the end fatal to their lives. Even in the day-time, tho' the ſpirit did not then appear, yet the impreſſion remained ſo ſtrong upon their imaginations, that it ſtill ſeemed before their eyes, and kept them in perpetual alarm. By theſe means the houſe was at laſt deſerted, as being deemed abſolutely uninhabitable; ſo that it was now entirely abandoned to the ghoſt. However, in hopes that ſome tenant might be found who was ignorant of this very alarming circumſtance which attended it, a bill was put up, giving notice that it was either to be let or ſold. It happened that Athenodorus the philoſopher came to Athens at this time, and reading the bill, enquired the price. The extraordinary cheapneſs raiſed his ſuſpicion; nevertheleſs, when he heard the whole ſtory, he was ſo far from being diſcouraged, that he was more ſtrongly inclined to hire it, and, in ſhort, actually did ſo. When it grew towards evening, he ordered a couch to be prepared for him in the fore-part of the houſe, and after calling for a light, together with his pencil and tablets, he directed all his people to retire. But, that his mind might not, for want of employment, be open to the vain terrors of imaginary noises and spirits, he applied himself to writing with the utmost attention. The first part of the night passed in usual silence, when at length the chains began to rattle: however, he neither lifted up his eyes, nor laid down his pencil, but diverted his observation by pursuing his studies with greater earnestness. The noise increased and advanced nearer, till it seemed at the door, and at last in the chamber. He looked up, and saw the ghost exactly in the manner it had been described to him: it stood before him, beckoning with the finger. Athenodorus made a sign with his hand, that it should wait a little, and threw his eyes again upon his papers; but the ghost still rattling his chains in his ears, he looked up and saw him beckoning as before. Upon this he immediately arose, and, with the light in his hand, followed it. The spectre slowly stalked along, as if encumbered with his chains, and turning into the area of the house, suddenly vanished. Athenodorus being thus deserted, made a mark with some grass and leaves where the spirit left him. The next day, he gave information to the magistrates, and advised them to order that spot to be dug up. This was accordingly done, and the skeleton of a man in chains was there found; for, the body having lain a considerable time in the ground, was putrified, and had mouldered away from the fetters. The bones being collected together were publicly buried: and thus, after the ghost was appeased by the proper ceremonies, the house was haunted no more. This story I believe upon the credit of others; what I am going to mention, I give you upon my own. I have a freed-man named Marcus, who is by no means illiterate. One* night as he and his younger brother were lying together, he fancied he saw some person upon his bed, who took out a pair of scissars, and cut off the hair from the top part of his head; in the morning, it appeared the boy's hair was actually cut, and the clippings lay scattered about the floor. A short time after, an event of the like nature contributed to give credit to the former

---

* Those who are unacquainted with the genius of the religion of ancient Rome, may be inclined to think meanly of our author's judgement, from this and the following story; but when it is remembered, that the greatest characters which we meet with among that illustrious people, are all strongly marked with a vein of superstition, no particular charge of weak credulity can with justice be brought from hence against Pliny. The truth is, it was a national turn, and countenanced by the constitution of their government, insomuch that omens, even of the lowest kind, were considered previous to every step either of foreign or domestic concern: and the wisest and gravest of their historians, the judicious Livy not excepted, have given into accounts of this nature. Even a noble historian among our own countrymen, has not scrupled to insert a relation of the same kind and credibility, in his history of the civil wars.

mer story. A young lad of my family was sleeping in his apartment with the rest of his companions, when two persons clad in white came in, as he says, thro' the windows, and cut off his hair as he lay; and having finished the operation, returned the same way they entered. The next morning it was found that this boy had been served just as the other, and with the very same circumstance of the hair spread about the room. Nothing remarkable indeed followed these events, unless that I escaped a prosecution, in which, if Domitian (during whose reign this happened) had lived some time longer, I should certainly have been involved. For, after the death of that emperor, articles of impeachment against me were found in his scrutore, which had been exhibited by Carus. It may therefore be conjectured, since it is customary for persons under any public accusation to let their hair grow, this cutting off the hair of my servants was a sign I should escape the imminent danger that threatened me. Let me desire you then maturely to consider this question. The subject merits your examination; as, I trust, I am not myself altogether unworthy to participate of the abundance of your superiour knowledge. And tho' you should, with your usual scepticism, balance between two opinions, yet I hope you will throw the weightier reasons on one side, lest, whilst I consult you in order to have my doubt settled, you should dismiss me in the same suspence and indecision that occasioned you the present application. Farewel.

LETTER XXVIII. *To* Septitius.

THERE are, it seems, certain persons who in your company have blamed me, as being upon all occasions too lavish in commendation of my friends. I not only acknowledge the charge, but glory in it; for, can there be a nobler error than an over-flowing benevolence? But still who are these, let me ask, that are better acquainted with my friends than I am myself? Yet grant there are any such, why will they deny me the satisfaction of so pleasing an error? For, supposing my friends deserve not the high encomiums I give them, certainly I am happy in believing they do. Let them recommend then this ungenerous discernment to those who imagine (and their number is not inconsiderable) that they shew their judgment, when they indulge their censure. As for myself, they will never persuade me that I can love my [a] friends too well. Farewel.

[a] Balzac with his usual happiness of allusion, observes, "Il y a des rivieres qui ne font jamais tant de bien que quand elles se debordent; de meme l'amitié n'a rien de meilleur que l'excès."

LETTER XXIX. *To* Montanus.

IT would raise your laughter first, and then your indignation, and perhaps, after having composed yourself a little, you would be inclined to laugh again, when you read what I am going to mention, and which you will scarcely credit without ocular inspection. I lately observed in the Tiburtine [a] road, near the first mile-stone, a monument erected to the memory of [b] Pallas, with the following inscription: THE SENATE DECREED TO HIM, AS A REWARD FOR HIS FIDELITY AND AFFECTION TO HIS PATRONS, THE HONOUR OF THE PRÆTORIAN [c] ORNAMENTS, TOGETHER WITH THE SUM OF FIFTEEN MILLION OF [d] SESTERCES: BUT HE WAS CONTENTED WITH ACCEPTING ONLY THE HONOUR. I am not indeed apt to wonder at distinctions of this sort, which are oftener the gift of Fortune than of Judgement; but I could not help reflecting, when I read this

---

[a] The road leading to *Tivoli*, in Campania.

[b] He was at first a slave in the court of Claudius Cæsar, who afterwards gave him his freedom, and raised him to his chief favour. The patrons mentioned in this Inscription, are, that emperor and his consort Agrippina, to whom Pallas had likewise recommended himself by some signal services.

[c] The senate, as a mark of honourable distinction, sometimes decreed the privilege of wearing the ornaments peculiar to certain dignities, to persons who had not enjoyed the office to which those ornaments were annexed.

[d] About 320,000 l. of our money.

this inscription, how contemptible and ridiculous are those honours, which are thus sometimes thrown away upon dirt and infamy; which such a rascal, in short, had the assurance both to accept and to refuse, and then set himself forth to posterity as an example of singular moderation! Yet why should it raise my indignation? rather let me treat it as a matter of derision, that persons of this vile character may not flatter themselves they have obtained any thing truly enviable, when their honours only expose them to severer ridicule. Farewel.

LETTER XXX. *To* GENITOR.

I AM extremely concerned to find that you have lost your pupil; a youth, as your letter assures me, of such great hopes. Can I want to be informed, that his sickness and death must have interrupted your studies, knowing, as I do, with what exactness you fill up every duty of life, and how warm your affection is to all those to whom you give your esteem? As for myself, the usual business of Rome pursues me to this place; and I am not out of the reach of people even here, who appeal to me either as their judge, or their arbitrator. Nor is this all: for, not only the farmers claim a sort of prescription to try my patience as they please by their continual complaints; but also the necessity of letting out my farms, gives me
much

much trouble, as it is exceedingly difficult to find proper tenants. For these reasons I can only study by snatches: still however I *do* study occasionally, and both compose and read by turns: but my reading teaches me, by a very mortifying comparison, with what ill success I attempt to be an author myself. Tho' indeed you give me great encouragement, when you compare the piece I wrote in vindication of *Helvidius,* to the oration of Demosthenes against Midias. I confess I had that harangue in my view: not that I was so vain and absurd as to pretend to rival it, but I endeavoured at least to imitate it, as far as the difference of our subjects would admit, and as nearly as a genius of the lowest rank can copy one of the highest. Farewel.

LETTER XXXI. *To* CORNUTUS.

CLaudius Pollio is extremely desirous of your friendship; and he deserves it, not only because he *desires* it, but because he offers you *his* in return; as indeed few ever request the one, without being disposed to give the other. He is an upright, honest, good-natured man, and modest, I had almost said, beyond measure; if indeed that virtue can be carried to excess. We served in the army together, when he commanded a troop of horse; and I had an op-

portunity

portunity of taking a nearer view of his character, than merely what his being my fellow-officer gave me. I was appointed by the lieutenant-general to examine the accounts of the several companies; and as I discovered many instances of gross avarice and neglect of duty in some, so I found the highest integrity and exactest care in Pollio. He was afterwards promoted to very considerable employments in the revenue; yet no temptations could corrupt the innate integrity of his soul, and no prosperity swell his breast with pride, but he preserved, in all the variety of posts thro' which he passed, his honour and his humanity unimpeached; to which I will add, he supported the fatigues of business with the same firmness of mind he now discovers in his retreat. He once indeed quitted his retirement for a short time, greatly to his credit; being called forth by my worthy friend Corellius to his assistance, in purchasing and dividing those lands which were given to the public by the liberality of the emperor [b] Nerva. And could there be any circumstance more to his honour, than to be thus particularly singled out as his coadjutor, by a person

[a] Nerva restored to the Romans all that Domitian had plundered them of; and gave a very large sum of money to be laid out in the purchase of lands for the support of decayed families.

son of so eminent a character as Corellius? You may judge how faithfully he reveres the sacred ties of friendship by the last wills [b] of several of his friends, particularly that of Musonius Bassus, a man of distinguished merit. Pollio (for he cultivates polite literature as well as every other valuable qualification) has very gratefully endeavoured to perpetuate and extend the memory of Bassus, by publishing an account of his life: a circumstance too uncommon and too generous, not to be particularly applauded; since the generality of the world seldom mention the dead, unless to complain of them [c]. Receive then this worthy man, greatly desirous (believe me) of your amity, with warm embraces, and even invite him to accept of it as what you owe him; for, he who makes the first advances towards friendship, cannot so properly be said to solicit as to claim a return. Farewel.

[b] See letter 20. of this book, note [b].
[c] Pliny seems to allude to the *Captatores*, or legacy hunters: a contemptible character extremely common among the Romans in the decline of their state, when the prevailing luxury of the times rendered too many of them, in order to supply their extravagance, capable of any meanness to obtain a pecuniary remembrance in the wills of their wealthy acquaintance, and too much mortified not to complain when they found themselves disappointed.

LETTER XXXII. To FABATUS.[a]

I Rejoice that the arrival of my friend Tiro was acceptable to you; but particulary, that you made use (as your letter informs me) of the opportunity which the presence of the proconsul afforded you, of manumizing [b] several of your slaves. For, as I wish to see our corporation[c] improved by every possible means, so particularly by an increase of citizens, as that, of all others, is the strongest ornament a community can receive. I am pleased too (not out of a spirit of vanity, however I confess I am pleased) with what you add, that both you and I were highly complimented, in the acknowledgments which were made upon this occasion; for, as Xenophon observes, *"the voice of praise is sweet;"* especially when we think we deserve it. Farewel.

LETTER XXXIII. To TACITUS.

I Strongly presage (and I am persuaded I shall not be deceiv'd) that your histories will be immortal. I ingenuously own therefore[d], I so much

the

---

[a] His wife Calphurnia's grandfather.
[b] See letter 16 of this book.
[c] Comum.
[d] As some ingenious writers have affected to draw a comparison between our author and Cicero, to the disadvantage of

the

the more earnestly wish to find a place in them. If we are generally careful to have our persons represented by the best artists, ought we not to desire that our actions may be related and celebrated by an author of your distinguished abilities? In view to this, I acquaint you with the following affair, which tho' it cannot have escaped your attention,

the former; it will not, 'tis hoped, be thought any want of reverence to a character, which deserves the highest veneration from every admirer of the fine arts, to set before the reader an instance, where Pliny greatly outshines that noble example he was, upon all occasions, so desirous of copying. There is a letter of Cicero extant for the same purpose as this of Pliny's, addressed to his friend Lucceius *, who was writing the history of his own times. The sensible Montaign condemns *both* as instances of immoderate ambition; and observes, that " † fortune, as it were in pure spight, has taken care to hand " down to us the vanity of these requests, while she has long " since destroyed the histories they solicited." Let it be remarked, however, in justice to our author, that upon a comparison of the two letters, the ambition of Pliny will appear far more reasonable than that of Cicero; for, the latter does not scruple to press his friend to transgress the rules of history, and break through the bounds of truth in his favour. *Te plane etiam atque etiam rogo, ut & ornes ea vehementius etiam quam fortasse sentis, & in ea leges historiæ negligas, amorique nostro plusculum etiam quam concedit veritas largire:* whereas Pliny, with a far nobler spirit, expressly declares he does not desire Tacitus to heighten the fact, and that actions of real worth need only to be set in their true light. In Cicero's letter, we read the extravagant dictates of the most immoderate ambition; and he himself confesses he had not the assurance to look his friend in the face while he expressed them: *Coram me tecum eadem hæc agere sæpe conantem deterruit pudor:* in Pliny's, we see nothing but what is agreeable to cool sense, and the honest ambition of one who was conscious he had acted well, and desirous posterity should know it.

* Ep. fam. l. 5. 12. † Tom. I. 329.

attention, as it is mentioned in the * public journals, still I acquaint you with it, that you may be the more sensible how agreeable it will be to me, that this action, greatly heightened by the hazard which attended it, should receive an additional lustre from the testimony of so bright a genius. The senate appointed Herennius Senecio, and myself, counsel for the province of Bœtica, in their impeachment of Bœbius Massa. He was condemned; and the house ordered his effects to be seized into the hands of the public officer. Shortly after, Senecio having learnt that

---

* Whether Pliny means by the *Publica acta*, the journal of the senate, or what * Tacitus and ‡ Suetonius call the *Diurna acta*, may admit of a doubt. The former seems to have been exactly in the nature of our Votes of the house of commons, wherein a short account was given to the public of what passed in the senate; the latter appears very much to resemble our Gazette, being an authorized narrative of the transactions worthy of notice which happened in Rome. Petronius has given us the form of the latter of these, in his account of Trimalchio; and as it may not, perhaps, be unentertaining to the English reader, to see how exactly a Roman news-paper runs in the stile of a modern one, the following is an article or two out of it.

" On the 26th of July, 30 boys and 40 girls were born at " Trimalchio's estate at Cuma."

" At the same time, a slave was put to death for uttering " disrespectful words against his lord."

" The same day, a fire broke out in Pompey's gardens, " which began in the night, in the steward's apartment." Petron. satyr. p. 196, ed. Var.

* Annal. 30, 31.   ‡ In J. Cæsar. 20.

that the confuls intended to fit to hear petitions, came to me, and propofed that we fhould go together, and addrefs them with the fame unanimity we executed the office which had been enjoined us, that they would not fuffer Maffa's effects to be diffipated by thofe who were appointed to preferve them. I anfwered, that as we had been counfel in this caufe by order of the fenate, I would recommend it to his confideration, whether it would be proper for us, after fentence had paffed, to interpofe any farther. " You are at liberty, faid he, to pre-
" fcribe what bounds you pleafe to yourfelf, who
" have no particular connections with the province,
" except what refult from your late fervices to
" them; but they have a much ftronger claim upon
" me, who was born there, and enjoyed the poft of
" Quæftor among them." If fuch, I replied, was his determined refolution, I was ready to attend him, that whatever refentment fhould be the confequence, it might not fall fingly upon himfelf. Accordingly we went to the confuls, where Senecio declared what he thought proper upon the occafion; to which I fubjoined a few words on my part. We had fcarcely ended, when Maffa, complaining that Senecio had not acted againft him with the fidelity of an advocate, but the bitternefs of an enemy, defired he might be at liberty to pro-

secute him for ᶠ treason. The whole assembly was struck with the utmost consternation and horrour at this motion. I immediately rose up; "Most
"noble

ᶠ The reader will undoubtedly be surprized to find a prosecution of *treason*, founded merely upon a suggestion of misconduct in the management of a private trial. But this difficulty will be cleared, perhaps, by considering the character of Domitian, in whose reign this transaction happened. To shew any dislike to those who were the favourites of that infamous emperor, was construed by him into an act of treason against himself. He could gather that poisonous weed (as our author in his panegyric strongly expresses it) even from the barren sands of the theatre *(crimina majestatis in arena colligebat;)* for not to admire even his gladiators, was deemed, in those wretched times, an act of disloyalty. If therefore Massa was in the good graces of Domitian it would have been very easy for the former, to strain the honest zeal which Senecio had shewn in conducting this cause, into an instance of disrespect to the emperor. And the character which Tacitus gives of this Massa strongly supports that supposition; for, he describes him as the bane of every good man, and an instrument of those calamities which the Romans suffered under Domitian; *optimo cuique exitiosus*, says he, *& in causas malorum quae tulimus.* [Tacit. hist. l. 4. 50.] It must be owned however, that the expression in the original *(postulatio impietatis)* does not so absolutely and necessarily imply, a prosecution of treason, but that it may admit of another interpretation. Accordingly, a gentleman of distinguished learning, who favoured the translator with his sentiments upon this passage, has offered a conjecture much too ingenious to be suppressed. "It was the practice (he observes) of the an-
"cients, that all deposits, trusts, sequestrations, wills, &c.
"should be lodged in the most secure and unsuspected places;
"accordingly they chose their temples for that purpose; and
"the priests were of course the legal sequestrators;

- Nos ibi apud Theotimum omne aurum deposuimus,
Qui illic sacerdos est in Diana Ephesia.

Plaut. Bacch.
"And

"noble consuls," said I, "I am afraid it should seem that Massa has tacitly charged me with having favoured him in this cause, since he did not think proper to join me with Senecio in the desired prosecution." This short speech was extremely well received by those who were present; as it soon afterwards got abroad, and was publicly mentioned with general applause. The late emperour Nerva (who tho' at that time in a private station, yet interested himself in every meritorious action which concerned the public) wrote an admirable letter to me upon the occasion, wherein he not only congratulated me, but the age, which had produced an example so much in the spirit (as he was pleased to call it) of better days. But, whatever the fact be, it is in your power to heighten and spread the lustre of it: tho' far am I from desiring you would in the least exceed the bounds of reality. History ought to be guided by strict truth; and worthy actions require nothing more. Farewel.

" And of this the classic and civil-law books furnish abundant
" proof. He thinks therefore, that an insinuation that Massa
" had been tampering with the church to betray this *fidei-*
" *commissum*, and that the security became suspicious, might
" *possibly* carry an action of *impiety*." However, upon a closer examination of the letter, and comparing it with the history of that age, the interpretation adopted in the text, may, perhaps, be justified.

THE LETTERS OF PLINY.

BOOK VIII.

LETTER I. *To* SEPTITIUS.

I Had a good journey hither, excepting only that some of my servants have suffered in their health by the violent heats. Poor Encolpius, my [a] reader, whose assistance is of such service to me both in my studies and amusements, was so affected by the dust, that it occasioned his spitting of blood: an acci-

---

[a] Persons of rank and literature among the Romans, retained in their families a domestic, whose principal business was to read to them.

accident which will prove not lefs unfortunate to me, than to himfelf, fhould he be thereby rendered unfit for thofe purpofes of literature in which he fo greatly excels. If that fhould unhappily be the event; where fhall I find one who will read my compofitions with fo much fpirit and fo captivating an elocution, or admire them with fo much feeling? But the gods feem to favour our better hopes, as his bleeding is ftopped, and his pain abated. He is extremely temperate on *his* part; and no attention is wanting on mine, nor any care on his phyfician's. Thefe confiderations, together with the falubrity of this air, and the quiet of retirement, give us reafon to expect, that the country will contribute as much to the reftoration of his health, as to his repofe. Farewel.

LETTER II. *To* CALVISIUS.

OTHER people vifit their eftates in order to recruit their purfes, but I go to mine only to return fo much the poorer. I had fold my vintage to the merchants, who were extremely eager to purchafe it, encouraged by the price it then bore, and what it was probable it would rife to: however they were difappointed in their expectations. Upon this occafion to have made one
genera

general undiftinguifhed abatement to all, would have been much the eafieft, but not the moft equitable method. I hold it particularly worthy of a man of honour, to be governed by the principles of ftrict equity in his domeftic as well as public conduct; in fmall, as in great affairs; in his own concerns, as well as in thofe of others: And if every deviation from rectitude is equally [a] criminal, every approach to it muft be equally laudable. In the firft place then, I remitted to all in general one eighth part of the price they had agreed to give me; that none might go away without a mark of my liberality: in the next, I particularly confidered thofe who having advanced to me large fums in part of payment, had done me fo much the more fervice, and had been the greater fufferers themfelves. To thofe therefore, whofe purchafe amounted to more than [b] ten thoufand fefterces, I returned (befide that which I may call the general and common eighth) a tenth part of what they had paid above that fum. I fear I do not exprefs myfelf with fufficient clearnefs; I will endeavour to explain my meaning: for inftance, fuppofe a man had purchafed of me to the value of [c] fifteen thoufand fefterces; I remitted to him one eighth part

---

[a] It was a doctrine maintained by the Stoics, that all crimes are equal.
[b] About 80 l. of our money.
[c] About 120 l. of our money.

of that whole fum, and likewife one tenth of [d] five thoufand. Befides this, as feveral had depofited, in different proportions, part of the price they had agreed to pay, whilft others had advanced nothing; I thought it would not be agreeable to equity, that all thefe fhould be favoured with the fame equal remiffion. To thofe therefore, who had made any payments, I returned a tenth part upon the fums fo paid. By thefe means, I made a proper acknowledgment to each, according to their refpective deferts; and likewife encouraged them, not only to deal with me for the future, but to be prompt in their payments. This inftance of my good-nature or my judgement (call it which you pleafe) was a very confiderable expence to me. However, I found my account in it; for, all the country greatly commended both the fingular generofity of thefe abatements, and the principle by which I regulated them. Even thofe to whom I did not *mete* (as the proverb is) *by the fame meafure,* but adjufted the remiffion to the fum they had advanced, held themfelves obliged to me, in proportion to the probity of their principles; and went away pleafed with having experienced, that not from me

[e] *The good and bad an equal boon receive.*

Farewel.

[d] About 40 l. fterling.
[e] Hom. Il. lib. 9. v. 319.

LETTER III. *To* Sparsus.

YOU tell me, that of all my works, the last I sent you is your greatest favourite. The same judgement has likewise been passed upon it by another of my very knowing and ingenious friends: and I am the more inclined to believe that neither of you is mistaken, not only as it is improbable you both should, but because I am much disposed to flatter myself, I always endeavour indeed, that my last performance may appear the most finished; and for that reason I prefer the speech I lately published, to that which you mention: I will send it you as soon as I can meet with a safe conveyance. And now I have raised your expectations of this piece, I doubt you will be disappointed when it comes to your hands. In the mean while, however, you may indulge the agreeable persuasion (and perhaps too without being disappointed) that it is a composition you will read with pleasure. Farewel.

LETTER IV. *To* Caninius.

I Greatly approve your design of writing a poem upon the [a] Dacian war: for where could you have chosen a recent subject so full of events, so extensive,

---

[a] Dacia comprehended part of the present kingdom of Hungary, together with part of Transilvania, Servia, Walachia

extensive, or indeed so capable of poetical ornament? a subject which, while it has all the marvellous of fiction, has all the recommendation of truth. You will sing of rivers taught to flow in new channels; of bridges ᵇ thrown over immense rivers; of encampments upon the dreadful precipices

chia and Moldavia. It was first subdued and added to the Roman empire by Trajan; in memory of whose victories over this nation, the famous pillar is supposed to have been erected, called *Trajan's pillar*, which is still to be seen entire at Rome. It is 128 Italian feet high, to the top of which you ascend by 184 steps, which wind round the inside. The outside is carved in basso relievo, with the representation of the most remarkable circumstances of this expedition. [Bartoli colonna Traj.] After the death of Trajan, his ashes were placed, as some authors say, in a golden ball on the top of this noble pillar: but Eutropius affirms they were deposited under it. Eutrop. l. 8. c. 5.

ᵇ It is probable Pliny here alludes to the famous bridge built by Trajan over the river Danube, in the upper Mœsia, that *last flight*, as Sir William Temple calls it, *of ancient architecture*. " It is stiled by the ancients, the most stately fa-
" bric of that nature in the universe. It was all of square
" stone, and contained 20 arches, each of them 120 feet
" above the foundation, and 60 feet in breadth, all distinct
" from each other 170 feet. It was built where the river was
" narrowest, and consequently where the stream was strongest
" and most rapid; which renders the fabric still more stupen-
" dous, on account of the almost insurmountable difficulties
" they must have met with in laying so large a foundation.
" The architect employed upon this occasion, was one Apol-
" lodorus of Damascus, who, it seems, left a description of
" this great work. We are told that some remains are still
" to be seen of it near Zeveria, in Lower Hungary —Adrian
" fearing the Barbarians might make use of it to invade the
" Roman territories, broke down the arches; but the piers
" were still standing in Dion Cassius's time, that is, 120 years
" after, though they served only to shew, says the writer,
" the utmost extent of human power: This stupendous fa-
" bric was begun and ended in a summer." Univ. Hist. v.
vi. p. 14.

cipices of craggy mountains; and of a brave ᶜ prince who, tho' driven from his palace, preferved his courage unfubdued to the laft moment of his life. You will defcribe too, the glorious victor's double triumph, one of which was the firft that was ever gained over that nation, 'till *then* invincible, as the other will be the laft. There is one difficulty however, and a very confiderable one it is, where to find expreffions equal to the fubject; a difficulty which feems almoft infuperable even by your elevated genius, tho' capable of rifing to the moft fublime topics. Some difficulty too you will find in reconciling thofe barbarous and uncouth names, efpecially that of the ᵈ king himfelf, to the harmony of Grecian numbers. There is nothing, however, fo hard that art and induftry cannot mitigate at leaft, if not abfolutely fubdue. If Homer is allowed to contract or lengthen, or change even Grecian names, which are nothing harfh to the ear, in order to make them run more fmoothly in his verfe; why fhould the fame liberty be refufed to you, efpecially fince it is neceffity,

ᶜ Decebalus, king of the Dacians, who rather than fall into the hands of the conqueror, or live in dependence, put an end to his own life.

ᵈ From hence Catanæus conjectures, upon the credit of Orofius, that the true name of the king was *Diurpaneus*, which was afterwards changed by the Greek and Latin writers, to Decebalus.

necessity, and not affectation, that pleads for the indulgence? Come on then, my friend, and after having, as poets are wont, invoked the gods, and among the rest, that divine hero*, whose mighty deeds and deep counsels you are going to celebrate, loosen all your cordage, spread every sail, and then, if ever, launch forth with the full flow of your unbounded genius:—for you must allow me to be poetical, when I am talking to a poet. And now I insist that you send me every part, as soon as it shall have received your last finishing touches; and even before, while it is only a rough sketch, and unformed embryo. You will tell me, that a detached portion cannot please, like one entire piece, nor an unfinished plan be as satisfactory as a complete work. I am sensible it cannot, and therefore shall consider it only as in its first rudiments: as a separate and disjoined member; and shall lay it up in my scrutore, to wait your last hand. Indulge me then with this very singular instance of your affection, and suffer me to be privy to what you would choose to conceal even from every other person. In a word, though the more time and caution you take in communicating your work to the public, the more, possibly, it may heighten my esteem and

approbation

* Trajan.

approbation of the poet, yet the sooner and with the less scruple you send it to me, the more I shall love and applaud the friend. Farewel.

LETTER V. *To* Geminius.

OUR friend Macrinus has received a most severe wound: He has lost his wife! a lady whose exemplary virtues would have rendered her an ornament even to former times. He lived with her thirty-nine years in the most uninterrupted harmony. How respectful was her behaviour to him! and how well did she herself deserve the highest respect! In her character were united all those amiable virtues that adorn and distinguish the different periods of female life! It should, surely, afford great consolation to Macrinus, that he has thus long enjoyed so exquisite a blessing. But that reflection seems only so much the more to imbitter his loss; as indeed the pain of parting with our happiness, still rises in proportion to the length of its continuance. I cannot therefore but be greatly anxious for so valuable a friend, till this deep wound to his peace shall be in a state to admit of proper applications. Time however, together with a satiety of grief itself, will best and indeed necessarily effect his cure. Farewel.

LETTER VI. *To* Montanus.

MY last letter has by this time, I suppose, informed you, that I observed lately upon a monument erected to the memory of Pallas, the following inscription: *The* [a] *senate decreed to him as a reward for his fidelity and affection to his patrons, the honour of the Prætorian ornaments, together with the sum of fifteen millions of sesterces: but he was contented with accepting only the honour.* I afterwards thought it worth while to search for the original record, and it run in a strain so very extravagant, that this proud inscription seems modest and humble, compared with the terms of the decree. The eulogiums which have been given to the most illustrious Romans, I do not say those of more remote antiquity, as the Scipios and the Mummii; but (to come nearer our own times) the Marii, the Syllas, and the Pompeys, fall infinitely short of those which have been lavished upon this man. Was it a spirit of banter, shall I suppose, or a principle of slavery that produced this decree? I would ascribe it to the former, were not raillery unbecoming the dignity of the senate. Must it be attributed then to be the most abject subjection?

---

[a] See B. 7. let. 29th, and the notes there.

subjection? Yet who is so wretchedly sunk as to be capable of such meanness! Or was it the lust of ambition that gave birth to this decree; and the mover of it in the senate proposed it, perhaps, with a view of paving the way to his own preferment? But whom can we suppose so irrational, as to desire to raise himself at the expence both of his own and the public honour, in a commonwealth where the only means to be first in rank was to be first in flattering Pallas? Not to mention their offering to a slave the Prætorian honours; they were slaves themselves who made the offer: not to animadvert upon that part of their decree, which says, that Pallas ought, not only to be intreated, but compelled to wear the [b] golden ring; no doubt it was not consistent with the dignity of the senate, that a person of Prætorian rank should wear an iron one: to pass over, I say, these less flagrant instances; mark, I beseech you, the following very extraordinary clause: *The senate* (and was it not expiated in form after so vile a pollution?) *the senate returns thanks to Claudius, not only for the honourable mention he himself was pleased to make of Pallas, but for the opportunity afforded the house also of testifying their benevolence towards him.* It was highly to the credit, no doubt, of the senate, not
to

[b] None but knights and senators had the privilege of wearing a gold ring; as an iron one was a badge of servitude.

to appear deficient in point of gratitude to Pallas! It goes on: *That Pallas, to whom every man acknowledges his obligations in the best manner he is able, may receive the just reward of his fidelity and singular services.* Would one not imagine that he had extended the bounds of the empire, or at least, rescued the armies of the state? But it proceeds: *since no occasion more agreeable could present itself to the senate and the Roman people, of exercising their liberality, than an opportunity of rewarding one who had proved himself so honest and disinterested a guardian of the emperor's finances.*—Such was the glorious ambition of the senate at that time; such the highest pleasure of the people; such the most agreeable occasion of exercising their liberality; to have an opportunity of exhausting the public treasures upon Pallas! It continues; *the senate therefore voted that fifteen millions of sesterces should be paid to him out of the treasury; and as he has a soul far above desires of this kind, that the emperor should be so much the more strongly intreated to use his authority with Pallas, to oblige him to comply with the inclination of the senate.* Nothing more indeed seemed wanting to complete this extravagant scene, than that the imperial authority should interpose; that Pallas should be pressed to yield to the desires of the senate; that Cæsar himself should be called upon to assist the house in opposing this inso-

insolent piece of self-denial, lest the humble Pallas should refuse fifteen millions of sesterces! He refused, nevertheless, the offer the public made him of this immense sum; the only thing he could possibly have done more arrogant than the accepting of it. Yet even this the senate applauded, and seem to lament in the following clause. *But whereas our excellent prince and father of his country has, at the instance of Pallas, expressed his desire to have that part of the vote withdrawn, which relates to the giving him fifteen millions of sesterces out of the treasury; the senate declares, that it was with much willingness and great justice they voted, among other honours, the said intended sum to Pallas, upon account of his fidelity and vigilance: however, in compliance with the emperor's desire, which they think cannot without impiety be opposed in any instance, they obey it even in the present.* Figure to yourself Pallas entering his protest, as it were, against the decree of the senate; moderating the honours which were offered him, and refusing, as something much more valuable, the fifteen millions, when at the same time he accepted the Prætorian ornaments, as a present of an inferiour nature. Represent to yourself, Cæsar yielding to the intreaties of his freed-man in the face of the senate, or rather indeed, obeying his commands; for in the present instance, to *intreat* was *to command!* Think of the senate declaring in every clause of this decree, that it was with great willingness and justice the house intended, among other honours, to present Pallas with this sum; and that it would have insisted upon his acceptance, but in compliance with the will of the emperor, which it was impious in any point to oppose! Was it owing then only to the obsequiousness of the senate, and the modesty of Pallas, that he did not receive fifteen millions out of the treasury? And was it in this instance, of all others, that they would have made an exception to their obedience, if they had thought it right to have done so in any? And now, after all this, you will imagine perhaps, that you are come to the end. Have patience however, there is still something more remarkable to follow: *And whereas it is highly expedient, that the generous disposition of the emperor to approve and reward merit, should be every where made known and celebrated, especially in such places where those who have the care and administration of his affairs, may be excited to an imitation; and whereas the approved fidelity and integrity of Pallas may stimulate others to emulate so laudable an example*—*It is therefore resolved, that the memorial which the emperor redde to the senate on the 28th of January last, together with the decree of the senate thereupon, shall be engraven in in tablets of brass, and hung up near the martial statue of* * *Julius Cæsar.* It was not, it seems, sufficient that the senate alone should be witness to this complicated disgrace; but the most frequented place in all Rome was chosen, in order to display it to the then present and future times: it was decreed, that all the honours of a most insolent slave, both those which he refused, and those which (as much as in the authors of the decree lay) he had borne, should be inscribed in brass: the Prætorian distinctions decreed to Pallas inscribed, like ancient treaties or sacred laws, upon public and everlasting monuments of brass! so great was their——I know not what epithet to give it——that the emperor chose to display his weakness, the senate their meanness, and Pallas his insolence, in the face of all the world! The senate was not ashamed to colour this turpitude with a shew of reason; and a noble one, in truth, it was, even *that others might be encouraged, by the rewards conferred upon Pallas, to a laudable emulation of his conduct!* Thus contemptible were all honours rendered, even those which the *noble* Pallas did not disdain to accept! And yet there were found persons of rank and birth, so humble as to desire and solicit those very honours which they saw thus offered by slaves and conferred upon

---

* In the Forum.

upon a freed-man. Happy for me that I was not born in those days, which I cannot help blushing for, as if I had actually lived in them! and I doubt not, they raise the same sentiments in you. I know the honest feeling of your temper, and am persuaded, that if I have been transported into a greater warmth of expression than is suitable, perhaps, to a private letter, you will think I have shewn rather too little, than too much indignation. Farewel.

LETTER VII. *To* Tacitus.

WHEN you sent me your treatise, it was not (as you were pleased to say yourself) as one master, or disciple, would communicate his works to another, but with the condescension of a preceptor to his scholar; for in that relation I must consider myself in respect to you. Accordingly you summon me to my studies, whilst I am a playing the truant and prolonging the Saturnalian [a] holidays.— Tell me now, could I have made you a more stiff and aukward compliment, or given a stronger proof, that I am so far from deserving to be your instructor, that I am not even worthy to be your pupil? However, I will venture to assume the character you have invested me with, and exert the

[a] Vol. I. p. 113. not. f.

the authority you have given me over your book: And with so much the more freedom, as I have nothing of my own to send you, upon which you may take your revenge. Farewel.

LETTER VIII. *To* ROMANUS.

HAVE you ever seen the source of the river [a] Clitumnus? As I never heard you mention it, I imagine not; let me therefore advise you to visit it immediately. It is but lately indeed I had that pleasure, and I condemn myself for not having viewed it sooner. At the foot of a little hill, covered with venerable and shady cypress trees, a spring issues, which gushing out in different and unequal streams, forms itself, after several windings, into a spacious bason, so extremely clear, that you may see the pebbles, and the little pieces of money which are [b] thrown into it, as they lie at the bottom.

---

[a] Now called *Clitumno:* it rises a little below the village of Campello in Ombria. The inhabitants near this river still retain a notion, that its waters are attended with a supernatural property, imagining it makes the cattle white that drink of it: a quality for which it is likewise celebrated by many of the Latin poets. See Addison's Travels.

[b] The heads of considerable rivers, hot springs, large bodies of standing water, &c. were esteemed holy among the Romans, and cultivated with religious ceremonies. *Magnorum fluminum* (says Seneca) *capita reveremur; subita & ex abdito vasti amnis eruptio aras habet; coluntur aquarum calentium fontes, & stagna*

tom. From thence it is carried off not so much by the declivity of the ground, as by its own weight and exuberance. It is navigable almost as soon as it has quitted its source, and wide enough to admit a free passage for vessels to pass each other, as they sail with or against the stream. The current runs so strong, tho' the ground is level, that the large barges which go down the river have no occasion to make use of their oars; while those which ascend, find it difficult to advance, even with the assistance of oars and poles: and this vicissitude of labour and ease, is exceedingly amusing when one sails up and down merely for pleasure. The banks on each side are shaded with great numbers of verdant ash and poplar trees, as distinctly reflected in the stream, as if they were actually existing in it. The water is cold as snow, and as lucid too. Near it stands an ancient and venerable temple, wherein is placed a statue representing the river-god Clitumnus in his proper vestment: and indeed the prophetic oracles here delivered, sufficiently testify the immediate presence of that divinity.

stagna quædam, vel opacitas, vel immensa altitudo sacravit. Ep. 41. It was customary to throw little pieces of money into those fountains, lakes, &c. which had the reputation of being sacred, as a mark of veneration for those places, and to render the presiding deities propitious. Suetonius mentions this practice, in the annual vows which he says the Roman people made for the health of Augustus. Suet. in vit. Aug.

divinity. Several little chapels are scattered round, dedicated to particular gods distinguished by different names, and some of them too presiding over different fountains. For, besides the principal spring, which is, as it were, the parent of all the rest, there are several smaller streams, which, taking their rise from various sources, lose themselves in the river; over which a bridge is thrown, that separates the sacred part from that which lies open to common use. Vessels are allowed to come above this bridge, but no person is permitted to swim, c except below it. The d Hispellates, to whom Augustus gave this place, furnish a public bath, and likewise entertain all strangers, at their own expence. Several villas, attracted by the beauty of this river, are situated upon its borders. In short, every surrounding object will afford you entertainment. You may also amuse yourself with numberless inscriptions, fixed upon the pillars and walls by different persons, celebrating the virtues of the fountain, and the divinity who presides over it. There are many of them you will greatly admire, as there are some that will make you laugh; but I must correct myself when I say so; you are

too

c The touch of a naked body was thought to pollute these consecrated waters, as appears from a passage in Tacitus, l. 14. Ann. c. 22.

d Inhabitants of a town in Ombria, now called Spello.

too humane, I know, to laugh upon such an occasion. Farewel.

LETTER IX. *To* URSUS.

IT is long since I have taken either a book, or a pen in my hand; since I have known the sweets of leisure and repose; since I have known, in short, that indolent, but agreeable satisfaction of doing nothing, and being nothing: so much have the affairs of my friends engaged me, and prevented me from enjoying the pleasures of retirement and contemplation. There is no sort of philosophical studies, however, sufficiently important to supersede the offices of friendship; for, they are offices, which philosophy herself teaches us most religiously to discharge. Farewel.

LETTER X. *To* FABATUS*.

YOUR concern to hear of my wife's miscarriage, will be equal, I know, to the earnest desire you have that we should make you a great-grand-father. The inexperience of her youth rendered her ignorant that she was breeding; so that

---
* His wife's grandfather.

that she not only neglected the proper precautions, but managed herself in a way extremely unsuitable to a person in her circumstances. But she has severely atoned for her mistake, by the utmost hazard of her life. Tho' you certainly will be afflicted to see yourself thus disappointed in your advanced age, of the immediate hopes of leaving a family behind you; yet it deserves your gratitude to the Gods, that in the preservation of your grand-daughter, you have still reason to expect that blessing: an expectation so much the more assured, as she has given this proof, tho' an unhappy one indeed, of her being capable of bearing children. These at least, are the reflections by which I endeavour to confirm my own hopes, and console myself under my present disappointment. You cannot more ardently desire to have great-grand-children, than I to have children; as the dignity of both our families seems to open to them a sure road to honours, and they will inherit the glory of descending from a long race of ancestors, whose fame is as extensive as their nobility is ancient. May we but have the pleasure of seeing them born, it will make us amends for the present mortification! Farewel.

LETTER XI. *To* Hispulla[a].

WHEN I consider that you love your niece even more fondly than if she were your own daughter, I ought in the first place to inform you of her recovery, before I tell you she has been ill; that the sentiments of joy at the one, may leave you no leisure to be afflicted at the other. Tho' I fear indeed, after your first transports of gratulation are over, you will feel some concern; and in the midst of your joy for the danger she has escaped, will tremble at the thought of that which she has undergone. She is now, however, in good spirits, and again restored to herself and to me; and is recovering her strength and health, as fast as she lost them. To say the truth, (and I may now safely tell it you) her life was in the utmost danger; not indeed from any fault of her own, but a little from the inexperience of her youth. To this must be imputed the cause of her miscarriage, and the sad experience she has had of the consequence of not knowing she was breeding. But tho' this misfortune has deprived you at present of a nephew, or a niece, to console you for the loss of your brother; you should reflect that
it

---

[a] His wife's aunt.

it is a blessing which seems rather to be deferred than denied; since *her* life is preserved from whom that happiness is to be expected. I intreat you then to represent this accident to your [a] father in the most favourable light; as your sex are the best advocates in cases of this kind. Farewel.

LETTER XII. *To* Minutianus.

I Beg you to excuse me this one day: Titinius Capito is to recite a performance of his, and I know not whether it is most my inclination, or my duty to attend him. He is a man of a most amiable disposition, and justly to be numbered among the brightest ornaments of the present age. He diligently cultivates the polite arts himself, and generously admires and encourages them in others; to many of whom he is the protector, the refuge, and the liberal patron; as he is to all of them a bright and exemplary model. In a word, he is the restorer and reformer of literature, now alas! well nigh sinking into total neglect and decay. His house is open to every man of genius who has any works to rehearse; and it is not *there* alone that he attends these assemblies with the most obliging good-

---

[a] Fabatus, grandfather to Calphurnia, Pliny's wife.

good-nature. I am sure at least he never once excused himself from mine, if he happened to be at Rome. I should therefore with a more than ordinary ill grace refuse to return him the same favour, especially upon so honourable an occasion. Should not I think myself obliged to a man, who, if I were engaged in any law-suit, generously attended the cause in which I was interested? And am I less indebted, now that my whole care and business is of the literary kind, for his assiduity in my concerns of this sort; which, if not the only, is however the principal instance wherein I can be obliged? But tho' I owed him no return of this nature; tho' I were not engaged to him by the reciprocal tie of the same good offices he has done me; yet not only the powers of his extensive genius, as elegantly polished as it is severely correct, but the dignity of his subject, would strongly incite me to be of his audience. He has written an account of the deaths of several illustrious persons, some of whom were my particular friends. It is a pious office then, it should seem, as I could not be present at their obsequies, to attend, at least, this (as I may call it) their funeral oration; which tho' a late, is however for that very reason, a more unsuspected tribute to their memories. Farewel.

LETTER XIII. *To* GENIALIS.

I Much approve of your having read my orations with your father. It is highly for your advantage to learn from a man of his eloquence, what to admire in compositions of this kind, and what to condemn; as you will at the same time be trained up in an habitual custom of speaking your real sentiments. You see whose steps it is you ought to follow; and happy are you in having a living example before you, which is at once the nearest and the noblest model you can pursue! In a word, that he whom nature designed you should most resemble, is, of all others, the person whom you should most endeavour to imitate. Farewel.

LETTER XIV. *To* ARISTO.

AS you are no less acquainted with the political law of your country, (which includes the customs and usages of the senate) than with the civil, I am particularly desirous to have your opinion, whether I was mistaken in an affair which lately came before the house. This I request, not with a view of being directed in my judgement as to what is passed, (for that is now too late) but in order to know how

how to conduct myself, if any case of the same nature should hereafter happen to arise. You will ask, perhaps, why I apply to you for information concerning a point, wherein I ought to be well instructed? But the tyranny of [a] former reigns, as it introduced a neglect and ignorance of all other parts of useful knowledge, so particularly of what relates to the customs of the senate; for who is there so idly industrious as to endeavour to learn, what he never can have an opportunity of practising? Besides, it is not very easy to retain even the knowledge one has acquired, where no occasion of exercising it occurs. Hence it was, that Liberty, at her [b] return, found us totally ignorant and inexperienced in what relates to her interest; and thus, in our eagerness to taste her sweets, we are sometimes hurried on to action, ere we are well informed in what manner it is proper we should act. But it was wisely provided by the institution of our ancestors, that the young men should learn from the old, not only by precept, but by their own observation, how to behave in that sphere, wherein they were one day themselves to move; as these, in their turn, transmitted the same mode of instruction to their children. Upon this principle it was, that the

[a] Those of Nero and Domitian.
[b] When Nerva and Trajan received the empire.

the youth were sent early into the army, that by being taught to obey, they might learn to command, and whilst they followed others, might be trained by degrees to become leaders themselves. And thus, when they were candidates for any office, they were obliged to stand at the entrance of the senate, that they might be spectators, before they were admitted parties in the public council of the empire. The father of each youth was his instructor upon these occasions; or if he were dead, some person of years and dignity supplied the place of a father. Accordingly they were taught by that surest method of discipline, Example, how far the right of proposing any law to the senate extended; what privileges a senator had in delivering his opinion in the house; the power of the magistrates in that assembly, and the rights of the rest of the members; where it is proper to yield, and where to insist; when and how long to speak, and when to be silent; how to distinguish and seperate complicated and inconsistent propositions [a], and how to improve upon another member's motion: in a word, they learnt by this means, whatever relates to the conduct

---

[a] If any opinion proposed to the Senate, was thought too general, and to include several distinct articles, some of which might be approved, and others rejected, it was usual to require that it might be divided: and this they sometimes did by a general voice of the assembly, crying out, *divide, divide,* Middlet. Treat. on the Roman Senate, 137.

conduct of a senator in the house. As for myself, it is true, I served in the army when I was a youth; but it was at a time when courage was suspected, and want of spirit honoured; when generals were without authority, and soldiers without modesty; when there were neither discipline nor obedience in the camp; but all was riot, disorder, and confusion; in short, when it was happier to forget, than to remember what one learnt. I attended likewise in my youth the senate, but a senate that was mute and dispirited; where it was dangerous to speak one's sentiments, and infamous to be silent. What satisfaction in learning, or indeed what could be learnt, when the senate sate in the utmost indolence, or acted with the highest infamy! when they were convened either for cruel or ridiculous purposes[a]; and when their deliberations were never

serious

---

[a] The fourth satire of Juvenal will serve as a comment upon this passage, where he acquaints us that a turbot of a most enormous size being presented to Domitian, he immediately convened the senate, in order to consult in what manner it should be dressed. The poet mentions the names of the persons who spoke in this remarkable debate, together with their several opinions upon a question so important, concluding his satire with this pathetic wish:

Atque utinam his potius nugis tota illa dedisset
Tempora sævitiæ, claras quibus abstulit urbi
Illustresque animas impune!—— Sat. 4.

Ah! as this day, that he had spent the rest,
And his dire reign had only been a jest!
Nor Rome her noblest blood had tamely seen
Flow unreveng'd!——

serious, tho' often sad. But I was not only a witness to this scene of wretchedness, as a spectator; I bore my share of it too as a senator, and both saw and suffered under it for many years; which so broke and damped my spirits, that they have not even yet been able fully to recover themselves. It is but within a short time (for all time seems short in proportion to its happiness) since we could take any pleasure in knowing what relates to, or in exercising the duties of, our station. Upon these considerations therefore, I may reasonably entreat you, in the first place to pardon my errour, (if I have committed one) and in the next, to lead me out of it by your superiour knowledge: for, I am sensible you have ever been diligent to inquire into the constitution of our country, both with respect to its public and private, its ancient and modern, its general and particular laws. I am persuaded indeed the point upon which I am going to consult you, is so singular, that even those whose great experience in public business, must have made them; one should suppose, acquainted with every thing of this nature, were either doubtful or absolutely ignorant in what manner to proceed. I shall be the more excusable, therefore, if I happen to have been mistaken; as you will gain so much the higher praise, if you can set me right in an affair, which it is not clear has ever yet fallen within your observation. The enquiry then before the house was, concerning the death of Afranius Dexter, who being found murdered, it was uncertain whether he fell by his own hands, or by those of his freedmen; and if the latter, whether they committed the fact in [b] obedience to the commands of Afranius, or were prompted to it by their own villainy. After they had been put to the torture, a certain senator (it is of no importance to mention his name, but if you are desirous to know, it was myself) was for acquitting them; another proposed that they should be banished; and a third that they should suffer death. These several opinions were so extremely different, that it was impossible either of them could stand with the other; and therefore in taking the votes, I thought they ought to be numbered separately. For, what is there in common between the opinion of those who deemed the accused deserved banishment, and those who were of opinion they merited death? certainly nothing more, than between those who voted

---

[b] Those who destroyed themselves, frequently made use of the hands of their slaves for that purpose. Thus Brutus and Cassius, after the loss of that fatal battle which decided the liberties of Rome, ran each of them upon the swords of their slaves. Florus, l. 4. c. 7.

voted for banishment, and the others who were for acquitting the prisoners. Tho' indeed he who was for discharging them, approached nearer to the sentiments of him who proposed exile, than the other who moved that they should suffer death: for both the former agreed at least in this, that their lives should be spared, whereas the latter were for a capital conviction. In the mean while, those senators who were for punishing with death, and those who proposed banishment, sate together on the same side of the house: and thus by a present appearance of union, covered their real disagreement. I moved therefore, that each of the three opinions should be separately voted, and that two of them should not, under favour of a short truce between themselves, join against the third. I insisted that such of the members who were for capital punishment should divide from the others who voted for banishment; and that these two distinct parties should not be permitted to form themselves into a body, in opposition to those who declared for acquittal, when they would immediately after disunite again: for it was not material that they agreed in disliking one of the proposals, since they differed with respect to the other two. It seemed very extraordinary, that he who moved that the freedmen should be banished, and the slaves suffer death,

death, should not be allowed to join these two motions in one, but that the question should be ordered to be put to the house in the disjunctive; and yet that the votes of those who were for inflicting capital punishment upon the freedmen, should be taken in conjunction with those who were for banishing them. For, if in the former instance, it was reasonable that the motion should be divided, because it comprehended two distinct propositions; I could not see why in the latter case, suffrages so extremely different should be thrown into the same scale. Permit me then, notwithstanding the point is already determined, to go over it again as if it were still undecided, and to lay before you those reasons at my ease, which I offered to the house in the midst of much interruption and clamour. Let us suppose there had been only three judges appointed to hear this cause, one of which was of opinion that the parties in question deserved death; the other that they should only be banished; and the third that they ought to be acquitted: should the two former unite their weight to overpower the latter, or should each be separately balanced? For, the first and second are no more compatible with each other than the second and third. They ought therefore to be counted in the senate as contrary opinions, since they were delivered as different ones. Suppose the same person had moved, that they should both have been banished and put to death; could they possibly, in pursuance of this opinion, have suffered both punishments? Or could it have been esteemed as one consistent motion, when it united two such different decisions? Why then should the same opinion, when delivered by distinct persons, be considered as one and entire, which would not be deemed so if proposed by a single man? Does not the law manifestly imply, that a distinction is to be made between those who are for a capital conviction, and those who are for banishment in the very form of words made use of when the house is ordered to divide? *You who are of such an opinion, come to this side; you who are of any other go over to the side of him whose opinion you follow.* Let us examine this form, and weigh every sentence: *You who are of this opinion*: that is, for instance, you who are for banishment, *come on this side*; namely, on the side of him who moved for banishment. From whence it is clear he cannot remain on the side of those who are for death. *You who are for any other*: observe, the law is not contented with barely saying *another*, but it adds *any*. Now can there be a doubt, whether they who declare

for a capital conviction are of *any* other opinion, than those who propose exile! *Go over to the side of him whose opinion you follow:* does not the law seem, as it were, to force those who are of different sentiments to contrary sides? Does not the Consul himself point out, not only by this solemn form of words, but by his hand and gesture, the place in which every man is to remain, or to which he is to go over? " But, it is objected, if
" this separation be made between those who vote
" for inflicting death, and those who are on the
" side of exile, the opinion for acquitting the
" prisoners must necessarily prevail." But how does that affect the parties who vote? Certainly it becomes not them to contend by every art, and urge every expedient, that the milder sentence may not take place. " Still, say they, those who
" are for condemning the accused, either capitally
" or to banishment, should first be set in opposi-
" tion to those who are for absolving them, and
" afterwards weighed against each other." Thus as in certain public games, some are by lot to engage with the conqueror; so, it seems, in the senate, there is a first and second combat, and of two different sentiments, the prevailing one has still a third to contend with. What? when any particular opinion is received, do not all the rest fall of course?

course? Is it reasonable then, that one should be thrown into the scale merely to weigh down another? To express my meaning more plainly: unless the two parties, who are respectively for capital punishment and exile, immediately separate upon the first division of the house, it would be to no purpose afterwards to dissent from those with whom they had joined before.—But I am dictating instead of receiving instruction.—Tell me then whether you think these votes should have been taken separately? My sentiments, 'tis true, prevailed; nevertheless I am desirous to know whether you think I ought to have insisted upon this point, or have yielded, as that member did who declared for capital punishment? For, convinced, I will not say of the legality, but at least of the equity of my proposal, he receded from his own opinion, and went over to the party for exile; fearing, perhaps, if the votes were taken separately (which he saw would be the case) the freedmen would be acquitted: For, the numbers were far greater on that side than on either of the other two, separately counted. The consequence was, that those who had been influenced by his authority, when they saw themselves forsaken by his going over to the other party, gave up a motion which they found abandoned by the first proposer, and deserted, if I may so express it, with their leader. Thus the three opinions terminated

terminated at length in two: and of thofe, one prevailed, and the other was rejected; while the third, as it was not powerful enough to conquer both the others, had only to choofe to which of the two it would yield. Farewel.

LETTER XV. *To* JUNIOR.

I FEAR I have over-loaded you by fending fo many volumes at once; but if I have, remember it was your own requeft. Befides, as you wrote me word you were likely to reap but little from the fruits of your vineyards, I imagined you would be at leifure to *reap* (as we fay) the *fruits* of learning. I have received the fame bad accounts of my own farms; and am therefore at leifure to compofe tracts for you, provided I can but raife money fufficient to furnifh me with good parchment. For fhould I be reduced to ufe the coarfe and fpongy fort, I muft either not write at all, or whatever I compofe, whether good or bad, muft neceffarily undergo one general blot! Farewel.

LETTER XVI. *To* Paternus.

THE sickness which has lately run thro' my family, and carried off several of my domestics, some of them too in the prime of their years, has deeply afflicted me. I have two consolations, however, which tho' they are not adequate to so considerable a loss, still they are consolations. One is, that as I have always very readily manumized my slaves, their death does not seem altogether immature, if they lived long enough to receive their freedom: the other, that I have allowed them to make a kind of will, * which I observe as religiously as if they were legally entitled to that privilege. I receive and obey their last requests, as so many absolute commands, suffering them to dispose of their effects to whom they please; with this single restriction, that they leave them to some of the family: which to persons in their station is to be considered as a sort of commonwealth. But tho' I endeavour to acquiesce under these reflections, yet the same tenderness which led me to shew them these indulgences, still breaks out and renders me too sensibly affected by their deaths.
However,

---

* A slave could acquire no property, and consequently was incapable by law of making a will.

However, I would not wish to be incapable of these tender impressions of humanity; tho' the generality of the world, I know, look upon losses of this kind in no other view, than as a dimunition of their property, and fancy by cherishing such an unfeeling temper, they discover superiour fortitude and philosophy. Their fortitude and philosophy, I will not dispute, but humane, I am sure they are not; for it is the very criterion of true manhood to *feel* those impressions of sorrow, which it endeavours to resist; and to admit, not to be above the want of, consolation. But perhaps I have detained you too long upon this subject,—tho' not so long as I would. There is a certain pleasure in giving vent to one's grief; especially when we pour out our sorrow in the bosom of a friend, who will approve, or, at least, pardon our tears. ^a Farewel,

---

^a There is something so uncommonly amiable in this *Family Piece*, that the reader cannot be displeased with being stopped a moment to take a second view of it. If nothing remained of Pliny, but this single *Trait* of his character, we might neverthelefs assuredly pronounce of him, that he was ennobled by every social virtue: for as it is certain the greatest minds have ever been most open to impressions of the humane kind; so every moral virtue necessarily flows from benevolence as from its true and genuine source. It is impossible that a man who has a just feeling of the calamities of others, can deliberately break thro' the moral ties of any kind; because it is certain he cannot do so, without being the occasion of suffering to those who stand within the influence of the particular action. This prin-

LETTER XVII. To MACRINUS.

IS the season with you as rude and boisterous as it is with us? All here is tempest and inundation. The Tiber has swelled its channel, and overflowed its banks far and wide. Tho' the wise precaution of the emperor had guarded against this evil, by cutting several outlets to the river; it has nevertheless flooded all the fields and vallies, and entirely overspread the whole face of the flat country. It seems to have gone out to meet those rivers which it used to receive and carry off in one united

principle also will ever afford the most unerring test of patriotism, or the public affections; for the cruel and unrelenting in private and domestic life, can never act upon the true notion of liberty, in the more enlarged relations of public concerns. With great justice therefore, our author makes this generous principle the evidence of real manhood; as Juvenal describes a tenderness of disposition to be the principal note of distinction, which nature has marked out between the rational and brute creation:

——————*Mollissima corda*
Humano generi dare se natura fatetur,
Quæ lachrymas dedit. Hæc nostri pars optima sensus.
——————*Quis enim bonus,*——
Ulla aliena sibi credat mala? Separat hoc
Nos a grege mutorum——————   Satyr. 15. 131.

Heaven gave the tear humane, a sign confest,
Soft pity dwells within the mortal breast;
That noblest passion noblest bosoms know!——.
Turn'd ever virtue from another's woe?
'Tis man's great privilege, the glorious line
That marks from brute, the human soul divine.

united stream; and has driven them back to deluge those countries, it could not itself reach. That most delightful of rivers, the [b] Anio, which seems invited and detained in its course by the charming villas that are situated upon its banks, has almost entirely rooted up and carried away the woods which shaded its borders. It has overthrown whole mountains, and in endeavouring to find a passage thro' the ruins that obstructed its way, has forced down houses, and risen over the desolation it has occasioned. The inhabitants of the hill countries, who are situated above the reach of this inundation, have been the melancholy spectators of its dreadful effects; having seen costly furniture, instruments of husbandry, ploughs, and oxen with their drivers, whole herds of cattle, together with the trunks of trees, and beams of the neighbouring villas, floating about in different parts,

---

[b] Now called the *Teverone*, which falls into the Tiber about three miles from *Rome*. The eloquent Balzac, speaking of a little river, has a thought which is celebrated by Bohours: * *Cette belle eau* (says he) *aime tellement ce pais, qu'elle se divise en mille branches, & fait une infinité d'isles & de tours, a fin de s'y amuser davantage.* But he is indebted to Pliny for all the merit of it, as it is plainly a copy from this passage: an observation by no means intended as a reflection upon the French writer, who has too many original beauties of his own to suffer from a discovery of those which are not: it is designed only to shew, that the most celebrated author in the epistolary way among the moderns, found advantage in conversing with Pliny.

* *Dict. sur la man. de bien pens. p.* 137.

parts. Nor indeed have thefe more elevated places themfelves, to which the waters could not rife, efcaped the calamity. A continued heavy rain, as deftructive as the river itfelf, poured down in torrents upon them, and has deftroyed all the enclofures which marked that fertile country. It has damaged likewife, and even overturned fome of the public buildings, where numbers have been miferably buried in the ruins. And thus thofe people, befides the lofs of their effects, have fuffered the additional misfortune of lamenting their friends. I am extremely uneafy, left this extenfive ruin fhould have fpread to you: I beg therefore, if it have not, you will immediately eafe me of my fears. And indeed, I defire you would inform me tho' it actually fhould; for the difference is not great between fearing a danger, and feeling it; except that the evil one feels has fome bounds, whereas one's apprehenfions have none. For, we can fuffer no more than what actually *has* happened, but we fear all that poffibly *may* have happened. Farewel.

LETTER XVIII. *To* Rufinus.

IT is a mistaken maxim too generally advanced, that a man's will is a kind of mirrour wherein one may clearly discern his genuine character. We have a late instance to the contrary in Domitius Tullus, who appears a much better man since his death, than during his life. After having artfully encouraged the expectations of those who paid court to him, with a view to be his heir, he has left his estate to his neice whom he adopted. He has given likewise several very considerable legacies among his grand-children, and also to his great-grand-son. In a word, he has shewn himself a kind relation throughout his whole will; which is so much the more to be admired, as it was not expected. This affair has been much the subject of conversation; some representing him as guilty of the basest falshood and ingratitude; and while they thus complain as if they were actually his disinherited kindred, their invectives betray the mean motives of the attentions they paid him: others, on the contrary, applauding him extremely for having disappointed the hopes of this infamous [a] tribe of men, whom, the manners of the age considered, it is but prudence to deceive. They add, that

---

[a] See Vol. I. p. 219. note [a].

that he was not at liberty to make any other will, and that he cannot so properly be said to have bequeathed, as returned, his estate to his adopted daughter, since it was by her means he became possessed of it. For, Curtilius Mancia, whose daughter Domitius Lucanus, brother to this Tullus, married, having taken a dislike to his son-in-law, devised his estate to this young lady, (who was the issue of that marriage) upon condition that Lucanus her father would ᵃ emancipate her. He accordingly did so, but she being afterwards adopted by Tullus her uncle, the design of Mancia's will was entirely frustrated. For, these two brothers having never divided their patrimony, but living together as joint-tenants of one common estate, the daughter of Lucanus, notwithstanding the act of emancipation, returned back again, together with her fortune, under

the

ᵃ That is, would make her free; for (as has been observed in the notes above) the power of a father over his children, was unlimited amongst the Romans. It extended not only to their fortunes, but their lives, and was even greater than what the laws allowed over their slaves; for if a master sold his slave, who afterwards obtained his freedom, the former owner had no farther claim; whereas, in the case of a son, the father's right was not absolutely extinguished by the sale, but if the son obtained his freedom, he again came under his dominion. This authority could not be wholly disannulled, till the son had been thrice sold, and as often recovered his liberty; it then entirely ceased. The law vested the same power likewise as fully in the adoptive father, as in the natural. Justinian observes, this authority was peculiar to the Romans, and allowed by no other nation whatsoever. Inst. l. 1.

the dominion of her father, in confequence of this
fraudulent adoption. It feems indeed, to have
been the fate of thefe two brothers, to be enriched
by thofe who had the greateft averfion to them.
For, Domitius Afer, by whom they were adopted,
left a will in their favour, which he had made
eighteen years before his death; tho' it was plain
he had altered his fentiments with refpect to the
family, becaufe he was inftrumental in procuring
the confifcation of their father's eftate. There is
fomething extremely fingular in the refentment
of Afer, and the good fortune of the other two;
as it was very extraordinary, on the one hand,
that Domitius fhould endeavour to profcribe the
man whofe children he had adopted, and on the
other, that thefe brothers fhould find a parent in
the very perfon that ruined their father. But
Tullus acted juftly, after having been appointed
fole heir by his brother, in prejudice to his own
daughter, to reftore to her this eftate which came
to him from Afer, as well as to devife to her
all the fortune which he poffeffed in common with
his brother. His will therefore deferves the higheft
commendation, as it is the dictates of nature, juftice,
and honour; having thereby returned his obligations to his feveral relations, according to their refpective good offices towards him. He has made an
equitable acknowledgment likewife to his wife, having

ing by his will given to that excellent woman, who patiently endured much upon his account, several delightful villas, besides a large sum of money. Indeed, she deserved so much the more at his hands, as she was greatly censured for her marriage with him. It was thought unworthy a person of her rank and merit, after having had a former husband by whom she had issue, to marry, in the decline of her life, an old man, merely for his wealth, and who was so sickly and infirm, that even had he passed the best years of his youth and health with her, she might well have been disgusted with him. He had so entirely lost the use of all his limbs, that he could not move himself in bed without assistance; and the only enjoyment he had of his riches, was to contemplate them. He was even reduced to the wretched necessity (and one cannot mention it without loathing as well as pity) of having his teeth washed and cleansed by others: in allusion to which he used frequently to say, when he was complaining of the indecencies, which his infirmities obliged him to suffer, that he was every day compelled to lick his servant's fingers. Still, however, he lived on, and was willing to accept of life upon these miserable terms. That he lived so long, was particularly owing indeed to the care of his wife, who, whatever reputation she might lose at first by her marriage, acquired great honour by her conduct towards him during its continuance.

Thus I have given you all the news of the town, where nothing is talked of but Tullus. It is expected his curiosities will shortly be sold by auction. He had such an abundant collection of antient statues, that he actually filled an extensive garden with them, the very same day he purchased it; not to mention numberless other antiques which stood neglected in a lumber-room.

Now, if you have any thing worth communicating in return, I hope you will not refuse the trouble of giving me the intelligence; not only as we are all of us naturally fond, you know, of news, but because interesting anecdotes afford examples which may be of use in respect to our own conduct. Farewel.

LETTER XIX. *To* MAXIMUS.

MY studies prove both an entertainment and consolation to me; and as there is no pleasure I prefer to them, so there is no uneasiness they do not alleviate. In this season therefore of dejection, occasioned by the indisposition of my wife, the dangerous sickness of some of my servants, and the death of others, I have recourse to my books, as to the sovereign consolers of my sorrows. It is true, indeed, they teach me a greater sensibility to misfortunes, but they teach me too how to bear them with more patience. It is an established rule with me, before I publish any of my productions, to consult the judgement of my friends, and especially yours. I request you, therefore, to examine with particular care, the performance I here send you, as I am afraid, the disquietude of my mind may have prevented me from giving it the attention I ought. For, though I could command my grief so far as to sit down to write, I was not sufficiently master of my heart to do so with ease and chearfulness: but if study naturally tends to compose the mind; the mind must be previously in a composed state to give a proper effect to our studies. Farewel.

LETTER XX. *To* GALLUS.

THOSE works of art or nature which are usually the motives of our travels, are often overlooked and neglected if they happen to lie within our reach; whether it be that we are naturally less inquisitive concerning those things which are near us, while our curiosity is excited by remote objects; or because the easiness of gratifying a desire, is always sure to damp it; or, perhaps, that we defer from time to time viewing, what we know we have an opportunity of seeing whenever we please. Be the reason what it may, it is certain there are several rarities in and near Rome,

Rome, which we not only have never seen, but have never so much as heard of; and yet if they had been the production of Greece, or Egypt, or Asia, or any other country which we admire as fruitful in wonders, they would long since have been the subjects both of our reading, conversation, and inspection. For myself at least, I confess, I have lately been entertained with a sight of one of these our indigenous singularities, to which I was an entire stranger before. My wife's grandfather desired I would look upon his estate near [a] Ameria. As I was walking over his grounds, I was shewn a lake that lies below them, called [b] Vadimon, which I was informed had several very extraordinary qualities attending it. This raised my curiosity to take a nearer view. Its form is exactly circular; there is not the least obliquity or winding, but all is regular and even, as if it had been hollowed and cut out by the hand of art. The water is of a clear sky-blue, tho' with somewhat of a greenish cast; it seems by its taste and smell impregnated with sulphur, and is deemed of great efficacy in all fractures of the limbs, which it is supposed to consolidate. Notwithstanding it is but of a moderate extent, yet the winds have a great effect upon it, frequently throwing it into violent commotions.

---

[a] Now called Amelia, an episcopal city in Ombria.
[b] Now called *Lago di Bassanello*.

commotions. No veffels are fuffered to fail there, as its waters are held ᶜ facred; but feveral floating ᵈ iflands fwim about in it, covered with reeds and rufhes, together with other plants which the neighbouring marfh and the borders of the lake produce. Thefe iflands differ in their fize and fhape; but the edges of all of them are worn away by their frequent collifion againft the fhore and each other. They have all of them the fame height and motion; and their refpective roots, which are formed like the keel of a boat, may be feen hanging down in the water, on which-ever fide you ftand. Sometimes they move in a clufter, and feem to form one entire little continent; fometimes they are difperfed into different quarters by the winds; at other times when it is calm, they float up and down feparately. You may frequently fee one of the larger iflands failing along with a leffer joined to it, like a fhip with its long-boat; or perhaps, feeming to ftrive which fhall out-fwim the other: then again they all affemble in one ftation, and afterwards

ᶜ See above, note ᵇ Let. 8. of this book.

ᵈ The credit of this account does not reft entirely upon our author: Pliny the elder mentions thefe floating iflands, [l. 2. 95.] and fo does Seneca, who accounts for them upon philofophical principles. [Q. N. l. 3. 25.] Varenius fays, that in Honduras, a province in America, there is a lake in which are feveral little hills planted with fhrubs, &c. toffed up and down by the winds. And he quotes Boethius the Scots hiftorian, who affirms, that in a large *Loch*, called *Lomond Loch*, in Scotland, there is a floating ifland, upon which cattle graze. See Varen. Geogr. vol. 1. p. 412.

wards joining themselves to the shore, sometimes on one side and sometimes on the other, cause the lake to appear considerably less, 'till at last uniting in the centre they restore it to its usual size. The sheep which graze upon the borders of this lake, frequently go upon these islands to feed, without perceiving that they have left the shore, 'till they are alarmed by finding themselves surrounded with water; and in the same manner when the wind drives them back again, they return without being sensible that they are landed. This lake empties itself into a river, which after running a little way sinks under ground; and if any thing is thrown in, brings it up again where the stream emerges.— I have given you this account, because I imagined it would not be less new, nor less agreeable to you than it was to me; as I know you take the same pleasure as myself, in contemplating the works of nature. Farewel.

LET.

LETTER XXI. *To* ARRIANUS.

NOTHING, in my opinion, gives a more amiable and becoming grace to our studies as well as manners, than to temper the serious with the gay, lest the former should degenerate into austereness, and the latter run up into levity. Upon this maxim it is, that I diversify my graver works with compositions of a lighter nature. I had chosen a convenient place and season for some productions of that sort to make their appearance in; and designing to accustom them early to the tables of the idle, I fixed upon the month of July [a],

which

---

[a] The months of July and August was a time of vacation to the Roman lawyers, the courts of justice being then shut up, that the farmers might not be interrupted in their harvest, by being obliged to attend their law-suits at Rome.

―――――― *messesque reversæ*
Dimisere Forum; nec jam tibi turba reorum
Vestibulo, querulique rogant exire clientes;
Cessat centeni moderatrix judicis hasta.
                      Statius Syl. l. 4. 50.

Returning harvest bids contention cease,
And through the wrangling Forum all is peace;
No teazing clients now besiege thy way,
Nor judges sage the solemn spear display.

Nevertheless the courts, as appears from this letter, were sometimes opened during this season of vacation, upon cases, perhaps, of particular emergency.

which is usually a time of vacation to the courts of justice, in order to read them to some of my friends at supper: and accordingly I placed a desk before each couch[a]. But as I happened that morning to be unexpectedly called away to attend a cause, I took occasion to preface my recital with an apology. I intreated my audience not to impute it to me as any want of due regard for the business to which I had invited them, that on the very day I had appointed to read my performances to some of my friends, (tho' indeed but few) I did not refuse my good offices to others in their law-affairs. I assured them, I would observe the same rule in my writings, and should always give the preference to matters of importance, before those of entertainment; to serious engagements, before amusing ones; and to the business of my friends, before my own. The poems I recited consisted of a variety of subjects in different measures. It is by such arts as these, we who dare not rely upon the single force of our genius, endeavour to avoid satiating our readers. In compliance with the earnest solicitation of my audience, I recited during two days successively; but not in the manner that several practise, by making a merit of passing over the less shining passages; on the contrary,

---

[a] The ancient Romans lay extended upon couches during their suppers, which were always in the evening, that time being the general hour of their principal meal.

contrary, I omitted nothing, and freely confessed it. I redde the whole, that I might correct the whole; which it is impossible those who only select particular passages, should do. The latter method indeed, may have more the appearance of modesty, and perhaps respect; but the former shews a greater ingenuousness, as well as a more affectionate disposition towards the audience. For, the belief that a man's friends have so much regard to him, as not to be weary upon these occasions, is a sure indication of the love he bears them. To say the truth, one has little obligation to an audience, if they assemble merely with a view to their own entertainment. He who had rather find his friend's performance correct, than make it so, is to be considered as a stranger, or one who is too indolent to give himself any trouble. Your friendship for me leaves me no room to doubt that you are impatient to read my book, even in its present very imperfect state; and so you shall, but not till I have made those corrections which were the principal inducement of my recital. You are already acquainted with some parts of it; but even those, after they shall have been polished (or perhaps spoiled, as is sometimes the case by too frequent revisals) will seem new to you. For when a composition has undergone various changes, it
acquires

acquires an air of novelty even in thoſe very parts which remain unaltered. Farewel.

LETTER XXII. To Geminitus.

HAVE you never obſerved a ſort of people, who tho' they are themſelves the abject ſlaves of every vice, ſhew a kind of malicious indignation againſt the immoral conduct of others; and are moſt ſevere to thoſe whom they moſt reſemble? yet, ſurely a lenity of diſpoſition, even in perſons who have the leaſt occaſion for clemency themſelves, is of all virtues the moſt becoming. The higheſt of characters, in my eſtimation, is *His*, who is as ready to pardon the moral errors of mankind, as if he were every day guilty of ſome himſelf; and at the ſame time as cautious of committing a fault, as if he never forgave one. It is a rule then which we ſhould upon all occaſions, both private and public, moſt religiouſly obſerve, " to be inexorable to our own failings, " while we treat thoſe of the reſt of the world " with tenderneſs, not excepting even thoſe who " forgive none but themſelves;" remembering always what the humane, and, *therefore*, as well as upon other accounts, the *great* Thraſea uſed frequently

quently to say: [a] *He who hates vice, hates mankind.* You will ask me, perhaps, who it is that has given occasion to these reflections? You must know a certain person lately—but of that when we meet—tho', upon second thoughts, not even *then*, left whilst I condemn and expose *his* conduct, I should act counter to that maxim I particularly recommend. Whoever therefore, and whatever he is, shall remain in silence: for, tho' there may be some use, perhaps, in setting a mark upon the man, for the sake of example; there will be more, however, in sparing him, for the sake of humanity. Farewel.

LETTER XXIII. *To* MARCELLINUS.

THE deep concern I am under for the death of Junius Avitus, has rendered me incapable either of business, study or amusement. He was invested with the [b] laticlave in my house; as in all

the

---

[a] The meaning of this maxim seems to be, that, as it is extremely difficult to separate the action from the man, we should not suffer the errors of the world to raise in us that acrimony of indignation, which if well examined, perhaps, will be oftener found to proceed from some secret principle of malice, than a just abhorrence of vice; *Satius est* (as Seneca observes) *publicos mores & humana vitia, placide accipere* · a general philanthropy and universal benevolence being the most genuine marks, by which virtue distinguishes those who are truly in her interest. If this sense be admitted, there is no need to suppose (with some of the commentators) that any mistake has crept into the text.

[b] See vol. i. p. 82. note [a].

the honours he solicited, he was constantly assisted by my interest. I will add too, his affection and esteem for me were so great, that he formed his manners, and regulated his conduct by my guidance and direction: a disposition extremely uncommon in the youth of this age; for, who among them will now deign to submit to the experience and authority of their superiors? They think themselves at once in full possession of all wisdom and knowledge; and without revering or imitating the virtues of any, imagine they are a sufficient example to themselves. But Avitus was of a far different turn; he shewed his wisdom, in believing there were some who had more; and discovered his knowledge, in his desire to learn. He was ever consulting his friends upon some point relating to his studies, or his conduct; and he always returned from them with advantage, either by the advice he received, or the disposition he shewed. With what respect did he treat Servianus, one of the most accomplished men of the age! Avitus knew how to value such uncommon merit, as well as to endear himself to him in his turn. Accordingly, when Servianus went lieutenant from Germany into * Pannonia, he attended him as Tribune; not so much in the character of his fellow-soldier, as of his friend and admirer.

* A very extensive province, comprehending part of Austria, Hungary, &c.

admirer. With what care and integrity did he execute the office of Quæstor under several consuls, who all esteemed him, not only as an useful and experienced officer, but as an easy and agreeable companion! With what zeal and application did he solicit this very ᵇ Ædileship, from the enjoyment of which he is now prematurely snatched! a reflection that gives a peculiar poignancy to my affliction for the loss of him. His unavailing labours, his fruitless assiduities, and the honour which he merited only, not enjoyed, are for ever in my thoughts. The circumstance of his having first put on the laticlave under my roof; the first and the last suffrage I ever gave him; the conversations we have had, and the consultations we have held, all return fresh upon my mind. I am struck with the most tender sorrow when I consider his youth, and reflect upon the irreparable loss his family has sustained; an aged parent; a young wife to whom he had not been married much above a year; an infant daughter just born; so many pleasing hopes,
so

ᵇ The Ædiles were at first two officers chosen out of the body of the commons, in order to assist the Tribunes in the discharge of some particular parts of their functions, the chief of which was the care of public edifices. Others were afterwards elected out of the nobility, to inspect public games, determine causes relating to the selling or exchanging of estates, to supervise the public stores of corn, and other provisions, &c. Ken. Antiq. p. 116, 117.

to many tender joys, all reversed and destroyed in one day! When he was just elected Ædile; when he had lately commenced a bridegroom; when he was newly made a father, he was suddenly snatched from the midst of these satisfactions; and has left behind him an honour untasted, a mother inconsolable, a widowed wife, and an orphan infant, who will have the misfortune of never having known her father! But what increases my tears upon this melancholy occasion is, that being absent when this accident happened, I never knew of his sickness, till I heard of his death; and had no time to prepare myself for this cruel stroke, by previously apprehending it!—Such is the present distress of my mind!—You must not wonder then that it is the whole subject of my letter; for I am not able, at present, to think or talk of any thing else. Farewel.

LETTER XXIV. *To* Maximus.

THE friendship I profess for you, induces me, not indeed to direct (for you are far above the want of a guide) but to remind you, however, of what you already know, and to admonish you carefully to observe and firmly

firmly to put it in practice; in other words, to know it to all the more useful purposes of knowledge. You will consider yourself as sent to that noble province, Achaia, the real and genuine Greece, where politeness, learning, and even agriculture itself, are supposed to have taken their first rise; as sent to govern a state composed of free cities; that is, to a society of men who breathe the spirit of true manhood and liberty [a]; who
main-

[a] " It is remarkable, that even after Greece was absorb'd
" in the Roman empire, and became a province to it under
" the name of Achaia, it did not lose with its power and so-
" vereignty, that lively sense and love of liberty, which was the
" peculiar character of that people, amongst whom the arts
" were produced and brought to perfection. The Romans,
" when they had subdued Greece, left that generous, brave,
" polite people, in possession of many of their rights and pri-
" vileges. And they maintained such an ardent zeal for
" liberty, that, to name no other instances of it, when the
" civil wars happen'd in Italy, the Athenians very warmly
" espoused the part of Pompey, who fought for the repub-
" lic: and after Cæsar was killed, they erected statues in
" honour of Brutus and Cassius, near to those of Harmodius
" and Aristogiton, their ancient deliverers. It was hence
" Greece, Athens in particular, after it was very much
" fallen and degenerated, continued still to be the metro-
" polis of sciences, the school of all the fine arts, the stan-
" dard and center of good taste in all works of genius, to
" Cicero's time, and long afterwards; insomuch, that Rome
" sent its most illustrious youth to be perfected there in po-
" lite literature, eloquence, philosophy, and all the ingenious
" arts and sciences; and the emperors who loved learn-
" ing, if they could not go to Greece and become scholars
" there, as some of them did, brought Greece to them by
" inviting and receiving into their palaces its most celebrated
" professors and artists, and even intrusting the education
" of their children with Greek masters. Now, their con-
" tinuing

maintained the rights they received from Nature, by courage, by virtue, by alliances; in a word, by civil and religious faith. Revere the Gods and Heroes their founders; the glory of their antient days; and even that very antiquity itself; for age, as it is venerable in men, is in states sacred. Honour them therefore for their deeds of old renown; for those which true, and (I do not scruple to add) which fabulous, history has recorded. Indulge them in the full exercise of their dignities, their privileges, and their very vanity. Remember, it was from this nation we derived our [b] laws; that she did not receive

ours

"tinuing to excel in the arts and sciences, to what else can
"it be attributed, but to this, that with some small remains
"of liberty, they retained the spirit of liberty, the love of
"it, and zeal for it? It was indeed in consequence of this
"alone, that they maintained, in some degree, even till
"Italy was quite over-run with barbarism, a sovereignty the
"Romans could not take from them; a sovereignty in
"science, arts, and good taste. 'Tis impossible to account
"for it in any other way: they preserved the arts in a very
"great degree, because they retained the spirit of liberty in
"a very extraordinary one." *Turnbull on ancient Painting*,
p. 100.

[b] About the year of Rome 300, that is, 452 years before Christ, embassadors were sent into Greece, to make a collection of such laws and customs as the wisdom of that polite people had established, particularly the famous ones of Solon. At their return, these laws were approved and confirmed, and, together with some additional ones, were engraven on ten tables of brass. Two other tables of laws were soon afterwards added to these, which together with the former, went by the name of the *twelve tables*, and were looked upon as the fountain of all law, public and private. *Liv. l.* 3. *c.* 31. *Ferriere Hist. des Loix civ. c.* 5.

ours by conquest, but gave us her own in consequence of our particular request. Remember, it is Athens that you approach; it is Lacedæmon you govern: and to deprive so renowned a people of the declining shadow, the remaining name of liberty, would be a hardship, would be even a barbarity of the severest kind. Physicians, you see, tho' with respect to diseases there is no difference between the free and the slave, yet treat persons of the former rank with more tenderness, than those of the latter. Reflect on the illustrious figure these cities once made; but so reflect, as not to despise them for what they now are. Far be pride and asperity from my friend; nor fear by a proper condescension, to lay yourself open to contempt. Can he who is vested with the power and bears the ensigns of authority, can *He* fail of meeting with respect, unless by pursuing base and sordid measures, and first breaking thro' that awful reverence he owes to himself? Ill, believe me, is power proved by insult; ill can terrour command veneration; and far more efficacious is affection in obtaining one's purpose, than fear. For terrour operates no longer than its object is present, but love produces its effects when the object is at a distance; and as absence changes the former into hatred, it raises the latter into respect. It behoves you therefore, (and I cannot repeat it too often) it behoves you well to confider the end of your office, and to reprefent to yourfelf how great and important is the adminiftration of governing a free ftate. For, what is more becoming our focial nature than well regulated government, or more valuable than liberty? How ignominious then muft his conduct be, who turns the firft into anarchy, and the laft into flavery? To thefe confiderations let me add, that you have an eftablifhed reputation to maintain: the fame you acquired by the function of the Quæftorfhip in ͨ Bythinia; the good opinion of the emperor; the credit you obtained when you were Tribune and Prætor; in a word, this very government, which may be looked upon as the reward of your former fervices; are fo many glorious weights which are incumbent upon you to fupport with fuitable dignity. The more earneftly therefore ought you to endeavour that it may not be faid you fhewed greater urbanity, integrity, and ability, in a rude province remote from Rome, than in one which lies fo much nearer to the capital; in the midft of a nation of flaves, than among a free people; that it may not be remarked, that it was chance, and not judgement, appointed you to this office; when your character was unknown and unexperienced, not tried and approved. For, it is a maxim which your reading and converfation muft have

^ ᶜrovince in Anatolia, or Afia the lefs.

have often suggested to you, that it is a far greater disgrace to lose the fame one has once attained, than never to have acquired it. I again beg you to be persuaded, that I did not write this letter as presuming to instruct, but to remind you. Tho' indeed if I had, it would have only been in consequence of the great affection I bear you; a sentiment which I am in no apprehension of carrying beyond its just limits: for, there can be no danger of excess where one cannot love too well. Farewel.

THE LETTERS OF PLINY.

BOOK IX.

LETTER I. *To* Maximus.

I HAVE frequently advised you, to be as expeditious as possible in publishing what you have written either in defence of yourself, or against Planta; or rather indeed (as the circumstances of the case demanded) what you drew up with both those views: but I particularly press this advice upon you *now* that I hear he is dead.' For tho' you redde this piece to several of your friends, and put it into the hands of others, yet I should be

extremely

extremely sorry, that the world should suspect you did not venture to compose till after his death, what it is most certain you had finished during his life. Let not the character my friend has acquired of firmness and resolution be called in question: as it will not, when both the candid and the malicious world shall know, that the death of your adversary did not give you the confidence of writing, but only anticipated the opportunity of publishing this piece. Thus you will avoid the imputation,

With coward joy to triumph o'er the dead[a]:

For what you wrote and actually recited before his death, will be considered as published during his life, provided you publish it soon. If therefore you have any other work upon your hands, let me intreat you to lay it aside, and give your last finishing touches to this performance. It seemed to me indeed, when I formerly redde it, to want no improvements; and so it ought to seem now to you, as neither the subject requires, nor the time will admit of longer delay. Farewel.

[a] Hom. Od. lib. 22.

LETTER II. *To* Sabinus.

YOUR request that I would write to you frequent and long letters, is very pleasing to me. If I have forborne to do so, it is partly in consideration of the important affairs in which you are employed; and partly from some very cold and uninteresting occupations of my own, which engage my thoughts, and damp my imagination. Besides, I have not a sufficient supply of matter for frequent letters; and am by no means in the same situation that Tully was, whom you point out to me as an example. He not only possessed a most enlarged genius, but the circumstances of the times wherein he lived, furnished him with a variety of noble occasions of exercising it. As for myself, you know (without my telling you) to what narrow limits I am confined, unless my letters were to turn upon the fictitious and pedantic topics of the schools. But when I consider you in the midst of arms and encampments, animated by martial music, or fatigued with toil and heat; how absurd would it be to talk to you upon such subjects? This is my apology, and I think it a reasonable one; however, I almost wish you would not accept it: for to reject the excuses of a friend upon such an occasion, be they ever so just, is an evident proof of a warm affection. Farewel.

LETTER III. *To* Paulinus.

MANKIND differ in their notions of supreme happiness; but in my opinion he truly possesses it, who lives in the conscious anticipation of honest fame and the glorious figure he shall make in the eyes of posterity. I confess, if I had not the reward of an immortal reputation in view, I should prefer a life of uninterrupted ease and indolent retirement, to any other. There seem to be but two points worthy our attention; endless fame, or the short duration of human life. Those who are actuated by the former motive must labour to attain it with the utmost exertion of their powers; while such as are influenced by the latter, should quietly resign themselves to repose, nor wear out a short life, as many we see do, in a painful course of ill-directed pursuits, and then sink at last into a total dissatisfaction both of themselves and of the world. These are my daily reflections, and I communicate them to you, in order to renounce them if you should not join with me in the same sentiments; as undoubtedly you will, who are ever meditating some worthy deed to render your name immortal. Farewel.

LETTER IV. *To* MACRINUS.

I Should fear you would think the oration which you receive with this letter, immoderately long, if it were not of such a nature as to require being divided into several sections; which consisting of distinct charges, have the appearance of so many separate speeches. Wherever therefore you begin or end, you may consider what follows, either as connected with what precedes, or making of itself a new subject: so that you may look upon it as very diffuse upon the whole, and yet as extremely concise with respect to its particular parts. Farewel.

LETTER V. *To* TIRO.

YOU are greatly to be applauded for the just manner with which, as I am informed (and I make very strict enquiry) you administer the government of your province; one principal branch of which is to distinguish merit in every degree, and so to gain the love of the lower rank, as to preserve at the same time the affection of their superiours. But it is an errour many have fallen into, that while they endeavour to avoid the appearance of favouring the great, they run into the contrary extreme,

treme, and incur the imputation of acting with ill manners, or ill nature: an errour which you are far from committing, I well know. However, I cannot forbear adding a caution to my praise, and recommending it to you, to conduct yourself in such a manner, as to preserve the proper distinction of rank and dignity. For to level and confound the different orders of society, is far from producing an equality among mankind; it is, in fact, the most unequal thing imaginable. Farewel.

LETTER VI. *To* CALVISIUS.

I Have spent these several last days in my study with the most pleasing tranquillity. You will ask how that can be possible in the midst of Rome? It happened to be the season of celebrating the [a] Circensian games; an entertainment for which I have not the least taste. They have no novelty, no variety to recommend them; nothing, in short, one would wish to be present at twice. It is the more surprizing therefore, that so many thousand people should be possessed with the childish passion of desiring often to see a parcel of horses gallop, and men standing erect in their chariots. If indeed, it
were

---

[a] These games were originally of Græcian extraction, but first introduced among the Romans by Romulus, in order to favour his design of carrying off the Sabine virgins: they consisted of horse and chariot races, &c.

were the swiftness of the horses, or the skill of the charioteers that attracted them, there might be some little pretence of reason on their side. But it is the *dress* they [b] favour; it is the dress that captivates them. And if in the midst of the course the different contenders were to change habits, their different partizans would change sides, and instantly desert the very same men and horses, whom they just before were eagerly following with their eyes as far as they could see, and shouting their names with all the warmth of vociferous exclamation. Such mighty charms, such wonderous power is there in the colour of a paltry tunic! and this in the sentiments, not only of the vulgar (more contemptible than the uniform they espouse) but even in the opinion of some grave personages. When I observe such men thus insatiably fond of so silly, so low, so uninteresting, so common an entertainment, I congratulate myself that I am insensible to these pleasures; and am glad to employ the leisure of this season upon my studies, which others throw away upon the most idle occupations. Farewel.

[b] The performers at these games were divided into companies, distinguished by the particular colour of their habits; the principal of which were the white, the red, the blue, and the green. Accordingly the spectators favoured one or the other colour, as humour and caprice inclined them. In the reign of Justinian a † tumult arose in Constantinople, occasioned merely by a contention among the partizans of these several colours, wherein no less than 30,000 men lost their lives.

† Procop. de Bell. Persic. l. 1.

LETTER VII. *To* ROMANUS.

I AM glad to find by your letter, that you are engaged in building; for I may now defend my own conduct by your example. I am myself occupied in the same sort of work; and since I have you on my side, who shall deny I have reason too? We are pretty much agreed likewise, I find, in our situations; and as your buildings are carrying on upon the sea-coast, mine are rising upon the side of the Larian lake. I have several villas upon the borders of this lake, but there are two particularly, in which as I take most delight, so they give me most employment. They are both situated like those at * Baiæ:

one

---

* Now called Castello di Baia, in Terra di Lavoro. It was the place the Romans chose for their winter retreat; and which they frequented upon account of its warm baths. Some few ruins of the beautiful villas that once covered this delightful coast, still remain; and nothing can give one a higher idea of the prodigious expence and magnificence of the Romans in their private buildings, than the manner in which some of these were situated. It appears from this letter, as well as from several other passages in the classic writers, that they actually projected into the sea, being erected upon vast piles sunk for that purpose. Virgil draws a beautiful simile from this custom, where he compares the massy spear which Turnus hurled at Bitias, to one of those enormous piles thrown into the Baian sea:

Qualis

one of them stands upon a rock, and has a prospect of the lake; the other actually touches it. The first,

> *Qualis in Euboico Baiarum littore quondam*
> *Saxea pila cadit, magnis quam molibus ante*
> *Constructum jaciunt ponto; sic illa ruinam*
> *Prona trahit penitusque vadis illisa recumbit;*
> *Miscent se maria, & nigræ attolluntur arenæ.*
>
> Æn. ix. 710.

> So from the Baian mole, whose structures rise
> High o'er the flood, a massy fragment flies;
> The rapid rolling pile all headlong sweeps
> With one vast length of ruin to the deeps;
> Thick boil the billows, and on every side
> Work the dark sands, and blacken all the tide.
>
> PITT.

Horace also, in one of his moral Odes, points out and exposes this amazing luxury of building:

> *Tu secanda marmora*
>   *Locas sub ipsum funus; & sepulcri*
> *Immemor, struis domos;*
>   *Marisque Baiis obstrepentis urges*
> *Summovere littora,*
>   *Parum locuples continente ripa.*
>
> Od. 18. l. 2.

> —You, with thoughtless pride elate,
> Unconscious of impending fate,
> Command the pillar'd dome to rise,
> When lo! thy tomb forgotten lies;
> And tho' the waves indignant roar,
> Forward you urge the Baian shore,
> While earth's too narrow bounds in vain
> Thy guilty progress would restrain.
>
> Mr. FRANCIS.

And here indeed, luxury seems to have reigned in her most licentious refinements of all kinds; while the principal amusement of the place consisted in sailing upon the gulph in gaily painted

first, supported as it were by the lofty [b] buskin, I call my *tragic*; the other, as resting upon the humble sock, my *comic* villa. They have each their particular beauties, which recommend themselves to me so much the more, as they are of different kinds. The former commands a wider prospect of the lake; the latter enjoys a nearer view of it. *This*, by an easy bend, embraces a little bay; the promontory upon which the *other* stands, forms two. *Here* you have a strait walk, extending itself along the banks of the lake; *there* a spacious terrace that falls by a gentle descent towards it. The former does not feel the force of the waves; the latter breaks them: from *that* you see the fishing-vessels below; from *this* you may fish yourself, and throw your line from your chamber, and almost from your bed, as from a boat. It is the beauties therefore these agreeable villas possess, that tempt me to add to them those which are wanting————But I

need

painted barks, accompanied with all the melting softness that exquisite wines, fine women, and rapturous music could inspire. There was something even in the natural, as well as artificial turn of the scene, which seemed formed to dissolve the mind into a state of softness and dissipation: insomuch, that Seneca, with all his stoical fortitude, durst not trust himself in it above a day. See Seneca, ep. 51.

[b] The buskin was a kind of high shoe worn upon the stage by the actors of tragedy, in order to give them a more heroical elevation of stature; as the sock was something between a shoe and slipper, and appropriated to the comic players.

need not aſſign a reaſon to you; who, undoubtedly, will think it a ſufficient one that I follow your example. Farewel.

LETTER VIII. *To* Augurinus.

WERE I to beſtow praiſe on *you* from whom I have received ſo much, I am afraid it would ſeem to proceed, not ſo much from my judgement, as my gratitude. Nevertheleſs I will not ſcruple to ſay, that I think all your productions are beautiful; eſpecially, you may be ſure, thoſe of which I am the ſubject. And the ſame reaſon will account both for their deſerving that character and for my thinking ſo: for, as on the one hand you ever ſucceed beſt when friendſhip inſpires you; ſo on the other, I always like moſt what flatters my vanity. Farewel.

LETTER IX. *To* Colo.

I Greatly admire the generous grief you expreſs for the death of Pompeius Quinctianus, as it is a proof that your affection for your departed friend, does not terminate with his life. Far different from thoſe who love, or rather, I ſhould more properly ſay, who counterfeit love to none but the living. Nor indeed even *that* any longer than they are

are the favourites of fortune; for the unhappy are no more the object of their remembrance, than the dead. But *your* friendship is raised upon a more lasting foundation, and the constancy of your affection can only end with your life. Quinctianus, most certainly, well deserved to meet with that generous warmth from his friends, of which he was himself so bright an example. He loved them in prosperity; protected them in adversity; lamented them in death. How open was his countenance! how modest his conversation! how equally did he temper gravity with gaiety! how fond was he of learning! how judicious his sentiments! how dutiful to a father of a very different character! and how happily did he reconcile filial piety to inflexible virtue, continuing a good son, without forfeiting the title of a good man!—But why do I aggravate your affliction by reminding you of his merit?—yet I know your affection for the memory of this excellent youth is so strong, that you had rather endure that pain, than suffer his virtues to be passed over in silence; especially by me, whose applause, you imagine, will adorn his actions, extend his fame, and restore him, as it were, to that life from which he is prematurely snatched. Farewel.

LETTER X. To Tacitus[a].

I Should be glad to follow your precepts; but there is such a scarcity of boars, that it is impossible to pay at the same time equal homage to Minerva and Diana, who, you think, ought to be jointly worshipped. I must content myself therefore with offering my single devotion to the former; and even *that* with some restriction, considering the heats of the season, and the privileged indolence of retirement. I composed, indeed, a few trifles in my journey hither, which are only worthy of being destroyed, as they are written with the same careless unstudied manner that one usually chats upon the road. Since I came to my villa, I have made some few additions to them, not finding myself in a humour to turn my thoughts to things of more conse-

---

[a] The learned Catanæus, with some other commentators, imagines this letter does not belong to Pliny, but is the answer of Tacitus to the 6th epistle of the first book. He supports this conjecture, indeed, by no authority; only thinks it falls in exactly with the letter, to which he supposes it an answer, and fancies he discovers something in the stile different from our author's manner. But upon a comparison of the two letters, there seems little reason to believe one is an answer to the other. And as to any difference of stile (if there really be any) which the translator confesses he has not penetration enough to discover, it is much too precarious an argument to have any weight in the case. The supposition of Casaubon seems more probable, who thinks this epistle might be occasioned by one from Tacitus, wherein he reminded Pliny of his own advice to him, in that letter to which Catanæus imagines this to be an answer.

quence. Thus my poems, which you suppose I am finishing with so much advantage amidst the silence and solemnity of woods and groves, are, in truth, wholly at a stand. But I have revised an oration or two; tho' that kind of business is so unpleasant, as rather to resemble rustic labours, than rural amusements. Farewel.

LETTER XI. *To* Geminus.

YOUR letter was particularly acceptable to me, as it mentioned your desire that I would send you something of mine addressed to you, to insert in your works. I shall find an occasion of complying with your request more proper than that which you propose; the subject you point out to me being attended with some objections; and when you consider it again, you will think so.—As I did not imagine there were any booksellers at [a] Lugdunum, I am so much the more pleased to learn that my works are sold there. I rejoice to find they maintain the same character abroad, which they raised at home; and I begin to flatter myself they have some merit, since persons of such distant countries are agreed in their opinion concerning them. Farewel.

[a] Lyons, in the Lyonois, a province of France.

LETTER XII. *To* JUNIOR.

A Certain friend of mine lately chaſtiſed his ſon in my preſence, for being ſomewhat too expenſive in the article of dogs and horſes. " And pray, (I aſked for him, when the youth was " withdrawn) did you never commit a fault your- " ſelf which deſerved your father's correction? " Are you not ſometimes even now guilty of " errors, which your ſon, were he in your place, " might with equal gravity reprove? Are not all " mankind ſubject to indiſcretions? And have we " not each of us our particular follies in which we " fondly indulge ourſelves?"

The great affection I have for you, induced me to ſet this inſtance of unreaſonable ſeverity before you, as a caution not to treat your ſon with too much rigour and auſterity. Conſider he is but a boy, and that there was a time when you were of the ſame age. In exerting therefore, the authority of a father, remember always that you are a man, and the parent of a man. Farewel.

LETTER XIII. *To* Quadratus.

THE pleasure and attention with which you perused the vindication I published of [a] Helvidius, has greatly raised your curiosity, it seems, to be informed of those particulars relating to that affair, which are not mentioned in the defence; as you were too young to be present yourself at that transaction. When Domitian was assassinated, a glorious opportunity, I thought, offered itself of pursuing the guilty, vindicating the injured, and advancing my own reputation. But amidst an infinite variety of the blackest crimes, none appeared to me more atrocious, than that a senator, of prætorian dignity, and invested with the sacred character of a judge, should, even in the very senate itself, lay violent hands upon a member [b] of that august assembly; upon one, who formerly had the honour of being consul, and who then stood arraigned before him. Besides this general consideration, I had likewise a particular intimacy with Helvidius, as far as it was possible to hold with one, who fearing the tyranny of the times, endeavoured to veil

---

[a] He was accused of treason, under pretence that in a dramatic piece which he composed, he had, in the characters of Paris and Oenone, reflected upon Domitian for divorcing his wife Domitia. Suet. in vit. Domit. c. 10.
[b] Helvidius.

veil the lustre of his fame, and his virtues, in obscurity and retirement. Arria likewise, and her daughter Fannia who was mother-in-law to Helvidius, were in the number of my friends. But it was not so much private attachments, as the honour of the public, a just indignation at the action, and the danger of the example if it should pass unpunished, that animated me upon this occasion. At the first restoration of [c] liberty, every man singled out his particular enemy, (tho' it must be confessed, those only of a lower rank) and in the midst of much clamour and confusion, no sooner brought the charge than procured the condemnation. But for myself, I thought it would have more the appearance of moderation as well as spirit, not to take advantage of the general resentment of the public, but to crush this criminal with the single weight of his own enormous guilt. When therefore the first heat of public indignation began to cool, and declining passion gave way to justice, tho' I was at that time under great affliction for the loss of [d] my wife, I sent to Anteia, the widow of Helvidius, and desired her to come to me, as my late misfortune

prevented

[c] Upon the accession of Nerva to the empire, after the death of Domitian.

[d] Our author's first wife: of whom we have no particular account. After her death he married his favourite Calphurnia.

prevented me from appearing in public. When she arrived, I acquainted her with my intention not to suffer the injuries her husband had received, to pass unrevenged; and desired her to consult with Arria and Fannia (who were just returned from exile) whether she and they would join with me in the prosecution. Not that I wanted, I said, an associate, but that I was not so jealous of my own glory, as to refuse to share it with them in this affair. She accordingly communicated this message to them; and they all agreed to the proposal without the least hesitation. It happened very opportunely, that the senate was to meet within three days. It was a general rule with me to consult, in all my affairs, with Corellius, a person of the greatest prudence and wisdom this age has produced. However in the present case, I relied entirely upon my own discretion, being apprehensive he would not approve of my design, as he was of a very indecisive and cautious temper. But altho' I did not previously deliberate with him, (experience having taught me, never to advise with a person concerning a question we have already determined, where he has a right to expect that one shall be decided by his judgement) yet I could not forbear acquainting him with my resolution at the time I proposed to carry it into execution. The senate being assembled, I came into the house, and begged I might have
leave

leave to make a motion: which I accordingly did in few words, and with general assent. When I began to touch upon the charge and point out the person I intended to accuse (tho' as yet without mentioning him by name) I was attacked on all sides. "Let us know, says one, who is the object of this "extraordinary motion? Who is it (asked another) "that is thus accused, without acquainting the "house with his name, and his crime? Surely "(added a third) we who have escaped the late "dangerous times, may expect now, at least, to "remain in security." I heard all this with great calmness, and without being in the least alarmed; such is the effect of conscious integrity; and so much difference is there with respect to inspiring confidence or fear, whether the world had only rather one should forbear a certain act, or absolutely condemns it. It would be too tedious to relate all that was advanced by different parties upon this occasion. At length the consul acquainted me, that I was at liberty to propose what I thought proper, when my turn should come to give my opinion upon the ᶜ order of the day. I thanked him for allowing me a liberty,

---

ᶜ 'Tis very remarkable, that when any senator was asked his opinion in the house concerning the business in agitation,
he

a liberty, which he never yet (I said) refused to any; and so sat down: when immediately the house went upon other business. In the mean while, one of my consular friends took me aside, and with great earnestness telling me he thought I had proceeded in this matter with more courage than prudence, used every method of reproof and persuasion, to prevail with me to desist; adding at the same time, that I should certainly, if I persevered, render myself obnoxious to some future prince. "And so be " it, (I returned) should he prove a bad one." He had scarce left me, when a second came up: " for God's sake, said he, what are you at-
" tempting? Why will you ruin yourself? Do
" you consider to what hazards you are exposed?
" Why will you presume too much on the pre-
" sent situation of public affairs, when it is so un-
" certain what turn they may hereafter take? You
" are attacking a man who is actually at the head
" of the treasury, and will shortly be consul. Be-
" sides, do you consider what credit he has, and
" with what powerful friendships he is support-
" ed?" Upon which he named a certain person, who (not without several unfavourable rumours)

he had the privilege of speaking as long as he pleased upon any other affair, before he delivered his sentiments on the point in question. Aul. Gell. lib. 4. c. 10.

mours) [a] was then at the head of a powerful army in the East. I replied,

"*All I've foreseen, and oft in thought revolv'd* [b] "and am willing, if fate shall so decree, to suffer "by acting an honourable part, provided I can "draw vengeance down upon a most infamous "one." The time for the members to give their respective opinions was now arrived. Domitius Apollinaris, the consul elect, spoke first; after him Fabricius Vejento, then Fabius Posthumius; Vectius Proculus next, (who married my wife's mother, and who was collegue of publicius Certus, the person on whom the debate turned) and last of all Ammius Flaccus. They all defended Certus, as if I had already accused him (tho' I had not yet so much as once mentioned his name) and entered upon his justification as if I had exhibited a specific charge. It is not necessary to repeat, in this place, what they respectively said, having related it in their own words in the speech above-mentioned. Avidius Quietus, and Cornutus Tertullius answered them. The former observed, "that it was extremely unjust not to hear "the complaints of those who thought themselves "injured; and therefore that Arria and Fannia
"ought

---

[a] Probably concerning his intentions to employ his credit with the army, to be proclaimed emperor either immediately, or on the death of Nerva.
[b] Æneid. lib. 6. v. 105.

"ought not to be denied the privilege of laying
"their grievances before the house; and that the
"point for the confideration of the senate was not
"the rank of the person but the merit of the
"cause." Then Cornutus rose up and acquainted the house, "that as he was appointed guar-
"dian to the daughter of Helvidius by the con-
"suls, upon the petition of her mother and her
"father-in-law, he thought himself obliged to
"fulfil the duty of his trust. In the execution
"of which, however, he would endeavour to set
"some bounds to his indignation, by following
"that great example of moderation which those
"excellent women [a] had set, who contented them-
"selves with barely informing the senate of the
"cruelties which Certus committed in order to
"carry on his infamous adulation. And there-
"fore, he would only move, that if a punish-
"ment due to a crime so notoriously known,
"should be remitted, that at least Certus might
"be branded with some mark of the displea-
"sure of that august assembly." Satrius Rufus
spoke next, and meaning to steer a kind of middle course, expressed himself with much ambi-
guity. "I am of opinion, said he, that great
"injustice will be done to Certus, if he is not
"acquitted (for I do not scruple to mention
"his

[a] Arria and Fannia.

"his name, since the friends of Arria and Fannia, as well as his own, have done so too) nor indeed have we any occasion to be solicitous upon this account. We who think well of the man, shall judge him with the same impartiality as the rest: but if he is innocent, as I hope he is, and shall be glad to find, I think this house may very justly deny the present motion, 'till some charge shall be proved against him." Thus, according to the respective order in which they were called* upon, they delivered their several opinions. When it came to my turn, I rose up, and using the same introduction to my speech as I have published in the defence, I replied to them severally. It is surprising with what an universal assent I was heard, even by those who just before were loudest against me: such a wonderful change was wrought either by the importance of the affair, the eloquence of the speech, or the resolution of the advocate. After I had finished, Vejento attempted to reply; but the general clamour not permitting him to proceed, " I hope, conscript fathers, ᵇ said "he,

---

* In the early times of the republic, the consul began by asking the opinion of the *Prince* of the senate, and the rest went on each according to his age. Under the emperors, their will served as a rule: for as the prince presided in the senate, he demanded the opinion of him first, whom he thought fit to do that honour: however, he more usually began with the consuls.

ᵇ The appellation by which the senate was addressed.

" he, you will not oblige me to implore the af-
" fiftance of the ᵇ Tribunes." Immediately the
tribune Murena cried out, " You have my leave,
" moſt illuſtrious Vejento, to go on." But ſtill
the clamour was renewed. In the interval, the
conful ordered the houſe to divide, and having
counted the voices, difmiffed the ſenate, leaving
Vejento in the midſt, ſtill attempting to ſpeak.
He made great complaints of this affront (as he
called it) applying the following lines of Homer
to himſelf:

¹ *Great perils, father, wait th' unequal fight;*
Thoſe younger champions will thy ſtrength o'ercome.

There was ſcarce a man in the ſenate that did not
embrace and kiſs me, and all ſtrove who ſhould
applaud me moſt, for having with the utmoſt
hazard to myſelf, revived a cuſtom ſo long diſ-
uſed, of freely confulting the ſenate upon affairs that
concern the honour of the public; in a word, for
having wiped off that reproach which was thrown
upon it by the other orders in the ſtate, " that
" the ſenators mutually favoured the members of
" their

ᵇ The tribunes were magiſtrates choſen at firſt out of the
body of the commons, for the defence of their liberties, and
to interpoſe in all grievances offered by their ſuperiours. Their
authority extended even to the deliberations of the ſenate.

¹ Diomed's ſpeech to Neſtor, adviſing him to retire from
the field of battle. Iliad. iii. 102. Pope.

"their own body, while they were very fe-
"vere in animadverting upon the rest of their
"fellow citizens." All this was transacted in the
absence of Certus, who kept out of the way,
either because he suspected something of this nature was intended to be moved, or (as was said
in his excuse) that he was really indisposed.
Cæsar, however, did not refer the examination
of this matter to the senate. But I succeeded
nevertheless, in my aim, another person being
appointed instead of Certus to the consulship,
while the election of his collegue to that office
was confirmed. And thus, the wish with which
I concluded my speech, was actually realized:
"may he be obliged, said I, to renounce under
"a [k] virtuous prince, that reward he received
"from an infamous one [l] !" Some time after,
I recollected, as well as I could, the speech I
delivered upon this occasion; to which I made
some additions. It happened (tho' indeed it had
the appearance of being somewhat more than
casual) that a few days after I had published
this piece, Certus was taken ill and died. I
was told that his imagination continually represented

[k] Nerva.
[l] Domitian; by whom he had been appointed consul elect, tho' he had not yet entered upon that office.

sented me as a man that was pursuing him with a dagger. Whether there was any truth in this rumour, I will not venture to assert; but for the sake of example, however, I wish it might gain credit. And now I have sent you a letter, which if you should think is as long as the defence you say you have redde, you must impute it to yourself, for not being contented with such information as that piece could afford you. Farewel.

LETTER XIV. *To* TACITUS.

THO' you are by no means inclined to self-admiration, yet, be assured, none of my writings are more sincerely the undissembled dictates of my real thoughts, than those of which you are the subject. Whether, indeed, Posterity will concern herself with either of us, I know not; but surely we deserve some small regard at least, I will not say upon account of our geniuses (that would be too vain a presumption) but from our industry, our labours, and that high reverence we feel for her. Proceed we then, my friend, in the course we have entered, which as it has conducted some to the brightest eminences of Fame,

so

so it has drawn forth many from silent obscurity into public notice and reputation. Farewel.

LETTER XV. To FALCO.

I Retired to my villa at Tuscum, with the hopes of passing my time here, at least, in my own way: but that is a privilege, I find, I am not to enjoy even here; so greatly am I interrupted with the importunate complaints and petitions of my tenants. I look over their papers with more reluctance than I examine my own; for, to confess the truth, it is with great unwillingness I review even these. I am revising, however, some little orations; an employment which, after a length of time has intervened, is but of a very cold and unentertaining kind. In the mean while, my domestic affairs are neglected as much as if I were absent. Yet I sometimes so far act the part of a careful master of a family, as to mount my horse and ride about my farms, instead of taking my exercise in the *gestatio*. As for you, I hope you will keep up your good old custom, and in return for this account of my rural occupations, let us country folk know what is going forward in town. Farewel.

ᵃ See p. 4. note ᶜ.

LETTER XVI. *To* MAMILIANUS.

IT is no wonder the chace you mention afforded you infinite pleasure, since " the number of " the slain (to use your own historical expression) " was not to be counted^a." As for myself, I have neither leisure nor inclination for sports of that kind: not leisure, because I am in the midst of my vintage; nor inclination, because it has proved an extreme bad one this season. However, I shall be able, I hope, to *draw off* some new verses, at least, if not new wine, for your entertainment, which (since you request them in so agreeable a manner) I will not fail to send you, as soon as they shall be thoroughly *settled*. Farewel.

LETTER XVII. *To* GENITOR.

I Have received your letter, in which you complain of being highly disgusted lately at a very splendid entertainment, by a set of buffoons, mummers, and wanton prostitutes, who were playing their antic tricks ^b round the tables. But

---

^a An expression frequent among the historians in their description of battles.
^b These persons were introduced at most of the tables of the great, for the purposes of mirth and gaiety, and constituted

Book IX.   OF PLINY.   161

But let me advise you to smooth your brow a little. It is true, I admit nothing of this kind at my

tuted an essential part in all polite entertainments among the Romans. It is surprizing how soon this great people deviated from their original severity of manners, and were tainted with the contagion of foreign luxury. Livy dates the rise of this, and other unmanly delicacies, from the conquest of Scipio Asiaticus over Antiochus; that is, when the republic had scarcely subsisted above a hundred and fourscore years. * *Luxuriæ peregrinæ origo*, he observes, *exercitu Asiatico in urbem invecta est*. This triumphant army caught, it seems, the contaminating diversions of the people it subdued; and at its return to Rome, scattered infection among their countrymen, which spread by slow degrees, till it effected their total destruction. Thus did eastern luxury revenge itself on Roman arms! It may be wondered, that Pliny should keep his own temper, and check the indignation of his friend's at a scene, which was fit only for the dissolute revels of the infamous Trimalchio. But it will not, perhaps, be doing justice to our author, to take an estimate of his real sentiments upon this point, from the letter before us. Genitor, it seems, was a man of strict, but rather of too austere morals for the free turn of the age: *emendatus & gravis: paulo etiam horridior & durior ut in hac licentia temporum*. [Ep. 3. L. 3.] But as there is a certain seasonable accommodation to the manners of the times, not only extremely consistent with, but highly conducive to the interests of virtue, Pliny, probably, may affect a greater latitude than he in general approved, in order to draw off his friend from that stiffness and unyielding disposition, which might prejudice those of a gayer turn against him, and consequently lessen the beneficial influence of his virtues upon the world. A late most ingenious author, who has greatly distinguished himself in several branches of useful and polite literature, has given us a representation of one of these buffoons, from an antique in his collection: to which the reader is referred for a stronger idea of the vitiated and low taste of those, who could receive from them any gratification. See *Middleton, Antiq. tab. 9. fig. 2.*

Liv. l. 39. c. 6.

my own house; I endure them, however, without shewing any dislike, when I meet with them in other people's. "And why then (you will be "ready to ask) not have them yourself? Because the gestures of the wanton, the pleasantries of the buffoon, or the extravagancies of the mummer, give me no pleasure, as they give me no surprize. It is my particular taste, you see, not my judgement, that I plead against them. And indeed, what numbers are there who think the entertainments in which you and I most delight, are no better than impertinent follies? How many are there, who as soon as a reader, a lyrist, or a comedian is introduced, either withdraw from the company, or if they remain, shew as much dislike to this kind of diversions, as you did at those *monsters*, as you call them! Let us bear therefore, my friend, with others in their amusements, that they, in return, may shew indulgence to ours. Farewel.

LETTER XVIII. *To* SABINUS.

WITH what care and attention you will read my works, and how perfectly treasure them in your memory, your letter is a sufficient proof. Do you consider then, what trouble

trouble you are bringing upon your hands, when you kindly entice me, by every friendly artifice, to communicate to you as many of them as possible? I cannot, certainly, refuse your request; but shall comply with it, however, at different intervals, and observe some kind of regular succession. For, I would not by too copious and too frequent a supply, over-burthen and confound a memory, to which I already owe so many acknowledgments; nor pour in upon it such a profusion at once, as to obliterate what it had before retained, in order to make room for what succeeds. Farewel.

LETTER XIX. *To* Rufo.

YOU have read, it seems, in a letter [a] of mine, that Virginius Rufus directed the following lines to be inscribed upon his tomb;

Here Rufus lies, who Vindex' arms withstood,
Not for himself, but for his country's good:

For which you blame him, and think Frontinus acted much more reasonably, in forbidding any monument whatsoever to be erected to his memory: and in the conclusion of your letter, you

desire

[a] To Albinus; see book 6. let. 10.

desire my sentiments upon each. I loved them both; but I confess I admired *him* most whom you condemn; and admired him to such a degree, that so far from imagining I ever should have occasion to become his advocate, I thought he could never be sufficiently applauded. In my opinion, every man who has acted a great and distinguished part deserves, not only to be excused but approved, if he endeavours to secure immortality to the fame he has merited, and is desirous also to perpetuate an everlasting remembrance of himself, by monumental inscriptions. Yet rarely shall you find a man, who had performed such great atchievements, so modestly reserved upon the subject of his own actions, as Virginius was. I can bear him witness (and I had the happiness to enjoy his intimate friendship) that I never but once heard him mention his own conduct; and that was, in giving an account of a conversation which passed between him and Cluvius: " You well know (said Cluvius to him) " the fidelity required in an historian; you will " pardon me therefore, I hope, if you should " meet with any thing in my works, that is not " agreeable to you." " O Cluvius, he replied, " can you be ignorant that what I performed, was " in order that every man might enjoy the liberty " of writing what he pleased ?" But let us compare

pare Frontinus with him in that very inftance, wherein you think the former difcovered a more modeft and unoftentatious difpofition. He forbade a monument to be erected to him, it is true; but in what words? " The expence of a " monument, fays he, is fuperfluous; the remem-" brance of me will remain, if my actions deferve " it." Is there lefs vanity, do you think, thus to proclaim to all the ª world that his memory would remain; than to mark upon a fingle tomb-ftone, in two lines, the actions one has performed? It is not, however, my defign to condemn your favourite, hero; I only mean to defend Virginius: and what argument can be more prevailing with you, than one drawn from a comparifon between him and the perfon you prefer? In my own opinion, indeed, neither of them deferve to be condemned, fince they both were animated with the fame ardent paffion for glory, altho' they purfued their object by different roads: the former, in defiring to receive thofe monumental honours he had merited; the latter, in feeming to defpife them. Farewel.

ª It appears from hence, that this was not a teftamentary direction, but a declaration in fome work which Frontinus had publifhed.

LETTER XX. To VENATOR.

THE longer your letter was, so much the more agreeable I thought it; especially as it turned entirely upon my works. I am not at all surprized you should find a pleasure in them, since I know you have the same affection for every composition of mine, as you have for the author.

The getting in of my vintage (which tho' it has proved but a slender one this season, is, however, more plentiful than I expected) particularly employs me at present. If indeed I can with any propriety say so, who only gather a grape now and then, visit the wine-press, taste the must in the vat, and saunter to my domestics ᵃ; who being all engaged without doors, have wholly abandoned me to my readers and my secretaries. Farewel.

LETTER XXI. To SABINIANUS.

YOUR freedman, whom you lately mentioned to me with displeasure, has been with me, and threw himself at my feet with as much
sub-

ᵃ The distinction in the civil law between the *servi Urbani & Rustici*, is alluded to in the original; but as we have not the same among us, it is not possible, perhaps, to preserve this allusion, with propriety, in an English translation.

submission as he could have shewn at yours. He earnestly requested me with many tears, and even with all the eloquence of silent sorrow, to intercede for him; in short, he convinced me by his whole behaviour, that he sincerely repents of his fault. I am persuaded he is thoroughly reformed, because he seems deeply sensible of his guilt. I know you are angry with him, and I know it is not without reason; but clemency can never exert itself more laudably, than when there is the most cause for resentment. You once had an affection for this man, and, I hope, will have again: in the mean while, let me only prevail with you to pardon him. If he should incur your displeasure hereafter, you will have so much the stronger plea in excuse for your anger, as you shew yourself the more exorable to him now. Concede something to his youth, to his tears, and to your own natural mildness of temper: do not make him uneasy any longer, and I will add too, do not make yourself so; for a man of your benevolence of heart, cannot be angry without feeling great uneasiness. I am afraid, were I to join my intreaties with his, I should seem rather to compel, than request you to forgive him. Yet I will not scruple even to unite mine with his; and in so much the stronger terms, as I have very sharply and severely reproved him, positively threatening never to interpose again in his behalf. But tho' it was proper to say this to him, in order to make him more fearful of offending; I do not say so to you. I may, perhaps, again have occasion to intreat you upon his account, and again obtain your forgiveness; supposing, I mean, his fault should be such as may become me to intercede, and you to pardon. Farewel.

LETTER XXII. *To* Severus.

I HAVE been much alarmed by the ill state of health of Passienus Paulus, as indeed I had many and just reasons. He has a most excellent and generous heart, of which I have the happiness to share the warmest friendship. In his writings he very successfully emulates the ancients, whose spirit and manner he has closely imitated and happily restored; especially that of Propertius, to whom he is no less related by genius, than by blood, as he particularly resembles that poet in his chief excellency. When you read his elegies, all that is elegant, tender, and pleasing, will conspire to charm you; and you will clearly discover they are animated with the congenial spirit of Propertius. He has lately made some attempts of the lyric kind, in which he as successfully copies the manner of Horace,

race, as he has that of the other poet juſt mentioned. You would imagine, were there ſuch a thing as kindred in genius, that the blood of Horace likewiſe flowed in his veins. He diſplays a moſt wonderful compaſs and pregnancy of imagination: when he deſcribes the paſſion of love, you perceive his heart is entirely poſſeſſed by the moſt tender ſentiments; when he paints the emotions of grief, you ſee his breaſt is penetrated with the deepeſt ſorrow; when he enters upon topics of panegyric, it is with all the ardour of the warmeſt benevolence; when he diverts himſelf with ſubjects of pleaſantry, it is in the ſpirit of the moſt agreeable gaiety; in ſhort, whatever kind of poetry he engages in, he executes it with ſuch a maſterly hand, that one would imagine it was the ſingle ſpecies to which he had applied himſelf. The dangerous indiſpoſition of ſuch a friend and ſuch a genius, occaſion'd as much anxiety to me as it did pain to him. But at length *he* is recovered, and *my* peace is reſtored: an event which deſerves your congratulation, not only for my ſake, but for the ſake of literature itſelf, which was expoſed to as great a hazard by his danger, as it will receive glory by his recovery. Farewel.

LETTER XXIII. To MAXIMUS.

IT has frequently happened when I have been pleading before the centumviri, that those venerable judges, after having preserved as much as possible the gravity and solemnity suitable to their character, have at length been forced, as it were, to break thro' all restraints, and have risen up, with one consent, in my applause. I have often likewise gained as much glory in the senate, as my utmost wishes could desire: but I never felt a more sensible pleasure than by an account which I lately received from Cornelius Tacitus. He informed me, that at the last Circensian games, he sat next to a certain person, who, after much discourse had passed between them upon various points of erudition, asked him if he was an Italian, or a provincial? Tacitus replied, "Your acquaintance with literature must have "informed you, who I am." "Pray then, is "it Tacitus or Pliny I am talking with?" I cannot express how highly I am pleased to find that our names are not so much the proper appellatives of men, as a kind of distinction for learning herself; and that eloquence renders us known to those, who would be ignorant of us by any other means. An accident of the same nature happened to me a few days ago. Fabius Rufinus, a person of distinguished merit, was placed next to me at table; and below him a countryman of his, who was just then come to Rome for the first time. Rufinus desired his friend to take notice of me, and entered into a conversation concerning the object of my studies: to whom the other immediately replied, " That " must undoubtedly then be Pliny." To own the truth, I look upon these instances as a very considerable recompence of my labours. Had Demosthenes reason to be pleased with the old woman of Athens exclaiming ª, " This is De-" mosthenes!" and may I not be allowed to congratulate myself upon the extensive reputation my name has acquired? Yes, my friend, I will rejoice in it, and without scruple confess that I do. As I only mention the judgement of others, not my own,

---

ª The story as related by Tully, is this: Demosthenes met an old woman carrying a pail of water, upon which she whispers to her companion, " This is Demosthenes!" I must not, however, conceal from the reader, that Tully condemns the Grecian orator for being pleased upon this occasion, and accounts for it in the true spirit of genuine philosophy *, *apud alios loqui videlicet didicerat, non multum ipse secum:* he had learnt the art of talking to others, but was unacquainted, it seems, with the most instructive of all arts, the art of *self-converse:* a little of this home-philosophy would have taught him, in the judgement of Tully, to rate *vulgar* admiration at a lower value.

* Tusc. l. 5.

own, I am not afraid of incurring the censure of vanity.[b]; especially from you, who, as you envy no

[b] Those who have formed their notions of *modesty* according to the false refinements in manners, which latter times have introduced, will take offence, probably, at the advantageous terms, in which Pliny here, and in some other passages of these letters, speaks of himself. But it will not be just to estimate our author's character, by maxims which have been received in the world long since he left it. It is most certain, that modesty, according to the idea the ancients had of it, did not (neither in the truth of things does it) forbid a man to speak well of himself, where he has merit to support the character he claims. True modesty consisted only (as indeed it ought only to consist) in being *ashamed* to commit any thing base and unworthy; any thing unbecoming the dignity of human nature; any thing in defiance of that reverence we owe to ourselves, and to that rank we hold in the order of rational beings: she was in short, the *custos virtutum omnium*, as Tully emphatically calls her, the guardian and protectress of the whole train of human virtues. Pliny, who often recommends *modesty* as one of the most shining virtues in others, could never have spoken thus favourably of his own merit, if it had been contrary to the received notions of that most amiable quality. And that it was not, is extremely evident from the whole tenour of antiquity in the article of self-commendation. Homer's Ulysses (to borrow the observation of a very polite and judicious critic) " calls himself the *wisest*
" of the Grecians, as his Achilles does not scruple to repre-
" sent himself the *best and most valiant* of them; and that
" too in a council of all the princes: Virgil has given us
" his approbation of both the one and the other, in making
" Æneas talk frequently of his own piety and valour. So-
" crates in Plato, is always brought in to his advantage; he
" himself quotes the oracle, which pronounced him to be
" the *wisest of men*. Xenophon represents Cyrus, upon his
" death-bed, as taking notice of the greatest beauty of his
" own character, his humanity; in a piece which every one
" knows was designed for the character of a perfect prince.
" Cæsar and the great Jewish writer of his own life frequently
" commend themselves: the greatest critic, as well as the
" greatest orator among the Romans, who so often reckons
" *Modesty* among the things which are most necessary toward
" rendering

no man's reputation, so you are particularly zealous for mine. Farewel.

LETTER XXIV. *To* Sabinianus.

I Greatly approve of your having, in compliance with my [a] letter, received again into your family and favour, a discarded freedman, whom you once admitted into a share of your affection. This placability will afford you, I doubt not, great satisfaction: it certainly at least has me, both as a proof that you are capable of being governed in your passion, and as an instance of your paying so much regard to me, as to yield either to my authority, or to my request. You will accept, therefore, at once, both of my applause and my thanks. At the same time I must advise you, to be disposed for the future to pardon the faults of your people, tho' there should be none to intercede in their behalf. Farewel.

" rendering a man great in his profession; how open and
" frequent is he in praising himself, and setting his own
" merit in a true light? But what puts this beyond dispute
" (and shews at the same time, that a just commendation of
" one's self may be very consistent with the greatest modesty)
" is to be found in the sacred writings, in which Moses says
" of himself, that he was the *meekest man upon earth*." Essay on Pope's Odys. pt. 1. 52.

[a] See Let. 21 of this book.

LETTER XXV. To Mamilianus.

THO' you complain of the crowd of military occupations which press upon you, yet, as if you were enjoying the most uninterrupted leisure, you read and admire, it seems, my poetical trifles; and not a little encourage me to persevere in amusing compositions of that kind. I begin, indeed, to pursue this sort of study, not only with a view to my diversion, but my reputation, since they have approved themselves to the judgement of a man of your dignity and learning, and what is more, of your sincerity. At present I have some business in the courts of law, which takes up a little of my time; but as soon as I shall have dispatched it, I will again trust my muse to your candid bosom. You will suffer my little doves and sparrows to take wing among your eagles [a], if you should have the same good opinion of them as they have of themselves; if not, you will kindly confine them to their cage and their nests. Farewel.

[a] Alluding to the Roman standard, which was an eagle fix'd upon the top of a spear.

LETTER XXVI. *To* Lupercus.

I Said once (and I think not improperly) of a certain orator of the present age, whose compositions are extremely regular and correct, but by no means animated and sublime, " His only fault " is, that he has none." Whereas he who is possessed of the true spirit of oratory, should be bold and daring; should sometimes rise above the precise limits of common rules; and frequently soar even to dangerous heights: for danger is generally near whatever is towering and exalted. The Plain, 'tis true, affords a safer, but for that reason a more humble and inglorious path: they who run, are more likely to stumble than they who creep; but the latter gain no honour by not slipping, while the former even fall with glory. It is with eloquence as with some other arts; she is never more pleasing, than when she risks most. Have you not observed what acclamations our rope-dancers excite, at the instant of imminent danger? Whatever is most surprizingly hazardous, or as the Greeks better express it, whatever is most *perilous*, most excites our admiration. The pilot's skill is by no means equally proved in a calm, as in a storm: in the former case he tamely enters the port, unnoticed

and

and unapplauded; but when the cordage cracks, the maſt bends, and the rudder groans, then it is that he ſhines, in all his glory, and is hailed as little inferiour to a ſea-god. The reaſon of making theſe obſervations is, becauſe, if I miſtake not, you have marked ſome paſſages in my writings for being tumid, exuberant, and over-wrought, which, in my eſtimation, are but adequate to the idea, or boldly ſublime. It is material therefore to conſider, whether your criticiſm turns upon ſuch points as are real faults, or only ſtriking and remarkable expreſſions. Whatever is elevated is ſure to be obſerved; but it requires a very nice judgement to diſtinguiſh the bounds between true and falſe grandeur; between a juſt and enormous height. To give an inſtance out of Homer, both of the grand and elevated ſtyle, in the following lines, which can ſcarcely, I imagine, have eſcaped any reader's obſervation;

Heav'n in loud thunder bids the trumpet ſound;
And wide beneath them groans the rending ground [a].

———Again,

Reclin'd on clouds his ſteed and armor lay [b].

So

---

[a] Iliad. xxi. 387. Pope's tranſ.
[b] Iliad. v. 356. ſpeaking of Mars.

So in this whole passage:

> *As torrents roll, increas'd by numerous rills,*
> *With rage impetuous down their echoing hills,*
> *Rush to the vales, and pour'd along the plain,*
> *Roar thro' a thousand channels to the main.*

It requires, I say, a very delicate hand to poise these metaphors, and determine whether they are too figurative and pompous, or truly majestic and sublime. Not that I think any thing which I have written or can write, admits of comparison with these. I am not extravagant enough to entertain so proud an opinion: what I would be understood to contend for is, that we should throw up the reins to eloquence, nor curb the spirited exertions

---

*Iliad. 4. v. 452. Pope's transl. It is with great judgement Pliny distinguishes between *grandeur* and *elevation*, which tho' they are sometimes confounded, are most certainly distinct. Grandeur seems to consist entirely in the sentiment, and is the first of the five species of sublimity which * Longinus has enumerated. The passage that admired critic quotes from the account which Moses gives of the creation, is of this kind: *God said, Let there be Light; and there was Light.* Here is nothing in the expression ornamented or elevated; the language is plain and simple, yet conveys to the mind the noblest idea of omnipotence that the utmost efforts of the strongest imagination can conceive. But when a sublime thought is cloathed (if I may so say) in all the graceful propriety of just figure, it then becomes elevated. The illustrations which our author produces from Homer, are of this sort, where greatness of sentiment is heightened by beauty of imagery.

* Sect. 8.

exertions of genius by too much reſtraint. But it will be ſaid, perhaps, there is a wide difference between orators and poets. As if Tully were not as bold in his figures as any of the poets! Not to mention particular inſtances from him, in an article concerning which, I imagine, there can be no diſpute; does [a] Demoſthenes himſelf, that model and ſtandard of true oratory, does Demoſthenes check and repreſs the fire of his indignation, in that well-known paſſage which begins thus: " Ye infamous flatterers, ye evil genii, &c. ?"— And again, " It is neither with ſtones nor bricks " that I have fortified this city, &c."—And afterwards; " I háve *thrown* up theſe *out-works* before " Attica, and pointed out to you all the reſources " which human prudence can ſuggeſt, &c."—And in another place; " O my countrymen, I ſwear by " the immortal Gods, that he is *intoxicated* with the " ſpirit of his own magnanimous actions, &c."— But what can be more daring and beautiful than that

---

[a] The deſign of Pliny in this letter is, to juſtify the figurative expreſſions he had employed, probably in ſome oration, by inſtances of the ſame warmth of colouring from thoſe great maſters of eloquence, Demoſthenes and his rival Æſchines. But the force of the paſſages which he produces from theſe orators, muſt neceſſarily be greatly weakened to a mere modern reader, ſome of them being only hinted at, as generally well known; and the metaphors in ſeveral of the others, have either loſt much of their original ſpirit and boldneſs, by being introduced and received in common language, or cannot, perhaps, be preſerved in an Engliſh tranſlation.

that long digreſſion, which begins in this manner:
" A terrible diſeaſe, O my countrymen, has ſeized
" upon all Greece, &c.?"—The following paſſage
likewiſe, tho' ſomewhat ſhorter, is conceived in the
ſame boldneſs of metaphor:—" Then it was I roſe
" up in oppoſition to the daring Pytho, who *poured*
" *forth a torrent* of menaces againſt you, &c."—
The ſubſequent ſtricture is of the ſame ſtamp:
" When a man has ſtrengthened himſelf, as Philip
" has, by rapine and wickedneſs, upon the firſt
" pretence that offers, at the firſt impolitic ſtep, be
" it ever ſo inconſiderable, *he briſtles up his mane,*
" *and ſeizes all,* &c."—So in the ſame ſtile with
the foregoing is this: —" *Railed off,* as it were,
" from the privileges of ſociety, by the concurrent
" and juſt judgements of the three tribunals in the
" city."—And in the ſame place: " O Ariſtogi-
" ton! you have *betrayed* that mercy which uſed
" to be ſhewn to offences of this nature, or rather
" indeed, you have wholly *deſtroyed* it. In vain
" then would you flee for refuge to a *port,* which
" you have *ſhut up,* and *choaked with piles.*"—He
had ſaid before; " I am afraid therefore, you ſhould
" appear in the judgement of ſome, to have *erected*
" *a public ſeminary* of faction: for there is a
" weakneſs in all wickedneſs, which renders it
" apt to betray itſelf!"—And a little lower; " I
" ſee none of theſe reſources open to him; but
" all

" all is *precipice, gulph*, and *profound abyss*."—And again : " Nor do I imagine that our anceſtors in-
" ſtituted thoſe courts of judicature, that men of
" his character ſhould be *planted* there ; but on the
" contrary, *eradicated*, that none may emulate their
" evil actions."—And afterwards : " If he is then
" the *artificer* of every wickedneſs, if he openly
" makes it his *trade and traffic*, &c."—And a thouſand other paſſages which I might cite to the ſame purpoſe ; not to mention thoſe expreſſions which Æſchines ſays, are not words, but *wonders*.— You will tell me, perhaps, I have unwarily mentioned Æſchines, ſince Demoſthenes is condemn'd even by him, for running into theſe figurative expreſſions. But obſerve, I intreat you, how far ſuperiour the former orator is to his criticizer, and ſuperiour too in the very paſſages to which he objects ; for in others, the ſtrength of his genius diſcovers itſelf ; in thoſe above quoted, the ſublimity of it ſhines out. But does Æſchines himſelf avoid that mode of rhetoric which he reproves in Demoſthenes ? " The orator," ſays he, " O ye Athe-
" nians, and the law, ought to *speak* the ſame
" language ; but when the *voice* of the law de-
" clares one thing, and that of the orator ano-
" ther, we ſhould give our vote to the juſtice of
" the law, not to the impudence of the orator."— And in another place: " He afterwards mani-
" feſtly

" festly discovered the design he had, of con-
" cealing his fraud under cover of the decree, hav-
" ing expressly declared therein, that the embassa-
" dors sent to the Oretæ gave the five talents, not
" to you, but to Callias. And that you may be
" convinced what I say is the truth (after having
" *stripped* the decree of its *gallies*, its *trim*, and
" its arrogant ostentation) read the clause itself."—
And in another part: " Suffer him not to *break*
" *cover* and *escape* out of the limits of the ques-
" tion." A metaphor he is so fond of, that he re-
peats it again: " But remaining firm and confi-
" dent in the assembly, *drive* him into the merits of
" the question, and observe well how he *doubles*."—
Is his stile more reserved and simple, when he says:
" But you are for ever *wounding* our ears, and are
" more concerned in the success of your daily ha-
" rangues, than for the salvation of the city."—
What follows is conceived in a yet higher strain of
figure: " Will you not expel this man as the
" common calamity of Greece? will you not seize
" and punish this *pirate* of the state, who *sails* about
" in quest of favourable conjunctures? &c."—
with many other passages of the like nature.

And now I expect you will make the same attacks
upon certain expressions in this letter, as you did upon
those I have been endeavouring to defend. The
rudder

rudder that *groans*, and the pilot compared to a *sea-god*, will not, I suppose, escape your criticism: for I perceive, while I am suing for indulgence to my former stile, I have fallen into the same kind of figurative diction which you condemn. But attack them if you please, provided you will immediately appoint a day when we may meet to discuss these matters in person: you will then, either teach *me* to be less daring, or I shall learn *you* to be more bold. Farewel.

LETTER XXVII. *To* LATERANUS.

I Have had many occasions to observe the power, the dignity, the majesty, and I will add too, even the *divine* efficacy there is in history; but I never met with so strong an instance of it as lately. An author had recited part of an historical performance, which he had drawn up with the utmost regard to truth, reserving the remainder for another reading. When behold! the friends of a certain person came to him, and earnestly conjured him not to recite the rest; so much were they ashamed to hear those actions repeated, which yet they did not blush to commit! The historian complied with their request; as he honourably might.

Nevertheless, both the history and the action still remain, and will ever remain and be read. It will be read too with so much the greater curiosity, as the publication is delayed: for nothing raises the inquisitive disposition of mankind so much, as to defer its gratification. Farewel.

LETTER XXVIII. *To* ROMANUS.

YOUR letters have at length reached me, and I received three at once; all most elegantly written, and in the warmest spirit of friendship; in short, such as I had reason to expect from you, especially after having wished for them so long. In one, you enjoin me the very agreeable commission of forwarding your letter to that excellent lady, the virtuous [a] Plotina: I have forwarded them.

In

---

[a] Plotina was consort to the emperor Trajan. Her virtues are celebrated by several historians, and our author draws a most amiable character of her in few words, in his noble [*] panegyric upon that prince. He represents her (and he could not give a higher idea of her merit) as worthy the choice of that excellent emperor; of a sanctity of manners worthy of ancient Rome; plain in her habit, modest in her equipage, and polite in her address. She greatly contributed, it is [†] said, to the wise choice which Trajan made of a successor; and Adrian, in gratitude for her good offices to him in that election, dedicated a magnificent temple to her memory, at Nismes in Languedoc: the remains of which are still to be [§] seen.

[*] Plin. Paneg. No. 83.   [†] Eutrop. L. 8. c. 6.
[§] Montfauc. Diar. p. 4.

In the same letter you recommend to me Popilius Artemisius; and accordingly I have performed his request. You tell me also your vintage has proved extremely moderate. That complaint, notwithstanding we are separated by such distant countries, is common to us both. Your second letter informs me, that you are employed in dictating and writing upon a subject, wherein you have me strongly in view. I am much obliged to you; and should be more so, if you would give me the pleasure of reading your performance. It is but just indeed, that as I communicate to you all my compositions, you should suffer me to partake of yours, even tho' they should turn upon subjects which concern others. You promise me in the close of this letter, that as soon as you shall be informed with certainty, in what manner I intend to dispose of myself, you will make an elopement from your family, and immediately fly to me: I am already preparing certain chains for you, which, when I have you here, you will by no means be able to break. I learn from your third, that my oration in behalf of Clarius has been delivered to you, and that it appears more full than when you heard it pronounced. It is so, I confess; for I afterwards very considerably enlarged it.

it. You mention having fent me another letter, which you fay was written with peculiar confideration, and defire to know if I have received it: I have not, but impatiently wait its arrival. In the mean while write to me by every opportunity, and pay me for this delay with intereft, which I fhall compute at the higheft rate: for tell me, can you expect I fhould acquit you upon cheaper terms? Farewel.

LETTER XXIX. *To* Rusticus.

AS it is better to excel in any fingle art, than to arrive only at mediocrity in feveral; fo, a moderate fkill in feveral is to be preferr'd, where one cannot attain to perfection in any. Upon this maxim it is, that I have attempted compofitions of various forts, as I could not expect to carry any particular one to its higheft excellency. I hope, therefore, when you read any performance of mine, you will confider it with that indulgence which is due to an author, who has not confined himfelf to a fingle fubject, but has ftruck out into different kinds of compofition. In every other fort of workmanfhip, the number pleads fome excufe for the deficiencies of the artift; and
fhall

shall works of literature, the most difficult of all others, be tried by a severer law? But whilst I am bespeaking your candour, am I not bringing my gratitude in question? For, if you receive these last pieces with the same indulgence that you have all my former, I have more reason to hope for your praise, than to sue for your pardon: your pardon, however, will be sufficient. Farewel.

LETTER XXX. *To* GEMINIUS.

YOU have frequently in conversation, and lately in a letter, commended your friend Nonius to me for his great liberality to certain particular persons: I shall join with you in applauding him, if his bounty is not confined to those only whom you mention. I would have *Him* who desires to shew himself influenced by a spirit of true generosity, be liberal to his country, his kindred, his relations, and his friends; his friends, I mean, in distress: not like those who chiefly bestow their presents, where there is the greatest ability to make returns. I do not look upon such men as parting with any thing of their own; on the contrary, I consider their bounties as only so many disguised baits, thrown out with a design of catching the property of others. Much of the

same

same character are those, who take from one man in order to bestow on another, and aim at a reputation for munificence by sordid means. The first and fundamental principle of genuine beneficence, is to be contented with one's own; and after that, to cherish and embrace all the most indigent of every kind, in one comprehensive circle of general benevolence. If your friend observes this rule in its full extent, he is entirely to be commended; if he only partially pursues it, still he deserves (in a less degree indeed, however, he deserves) praise: so uncommon is it to meet with an instance of generosity even of the most imperfect kind! The lust of avarice has so totally seized upon mankind, that their wealth seems rather to possess them, than they to possess their wealth. Farewel.

LETTER XXXI. *To* Sardus.

I Still continued to enjoy your company, even after we had parted; for I entertained myself with reading your book. And I frequently perused, with particular complacency, (I honestly own it) those passages of which I am the subject: a subject upon which, indeed, you have been extremely copious. With what a variety of expression, and in how many different lights have you placed the same

ſame ſentiments concerning the ſame perſon? Will you ſuffer me to mingle my applauſes with my acknowledgments? I can do neither, ſufficiently; and if I could, there would be ſomewhat, I fear, of vanity, in making that perſon the ſubject of my praiſe, which is, in truth, the object of my thanks. I will only add then, that I thought your compliments to me raiſed the merit of your performance; as the merit of your performance heightened the pleaſure of your compliments. Farewel.

LETTER XXXII. *To* TITIANUS.

WHAT are you doing? And what do you propoſe to do? as for myſelf, I paſs my life in the moſt agreeable, that is, in the moſt diſengaged manner imaginable. I do not find myſelf therefore in the humour to write a long letter, tho' I am to read one. I am too much a man of indolence for the former, and juſt idle enough for the latter: for none are more indolent, you know, than your fine gentlemen, or have more curioſity than thoſe who have nothing to do. Farewel.

LETTER XXXIII. *To* CANINIUS.

I Have met with a story, which tho' it is authenticated by undoubted evidence, has all the air of fable, and would afford a very proper subject for the exercise of your truly poetical and sublime genius. It was related to me the other day at table, where the conversation happened to turn upon various kinds of extraordinary events. The person who gave the account, was a man of unsuspected veracity:—but what has a poet to do with truth? However, you might venture to rely upon his testimony, even tho' you had the character of a faithful historian to support. There is in Africa a town called Hippo, situated not far from the sea-coast: it stands upon a navigable lake, from whence a river runs into the main ocean, and ebbs and flows with the sea. Persons of all ages divert themselves here with fishing, sailing or swimming; especially boys, whom love of play and idleness bring hither. The contest among them is, who shall have the glory of swimming farthest; and he that leaves the shore and his companions at the greatest distance, gains the victory. It happened in one of these trials of skill, that a certain boy, more bold than the rest, launched out towards the
opposite

opposite shore. He was met by a dolphin[a], who sometimes swam before him, and sometimes behind him, then played round him, and at last took him upon his back, then set him down, and afterwards took him up again; and thus he carried the poor frighted boy out into the deepest part; when immediately he turns back again to the shore, and lands him among his companions. The fame of this remarkable event spread thro' the town, and crowds of people flocked round the boy (whom they viewed as a kind of prodigy) to ask him questions and hear him relate the story. The next day the shore was lined with multitudes of spectators, all attentively contemplating the ocean, and (what indeed is almost itself an ocean) the lake. In the mean while the boys swam as usual, and among the rest, the youth I am speaking of went into the lake but with more caution than before. The dolphin again appeared and came to the boy, who together with his companions swam away with the utmost precipitation. The dolphin, as it were, to invite and recal them, leaped and dived up and down, darting about in a thousand different convolutions. This he practised for several days together,

---

[a] This animal is celebrated by several of the ancients for its philanthropy, and Pliny the elder in particular, relates this very story, among other instances, in confirmation of that notion. See Plin. hist. nat. l. 9. c. 8.

ther, till the people (accuſtomed from their infancy to the ſea) began to be aſhamed of their timidity. They ventured, therefore, to advance nearer, playing with him and calling him to them, while he, in return, ſuffered himſelf to be touched and ſtroked. Uſe rendered them more courageous: the boy, in particular, who firſt had experienced the ſafety, ſwam by the ſide of him, and leaping upon his back, was carried about in that manner: thus they gradually became acquainted and delighted with each other. There ſeemed now, indeed, to be no fear on either ſide, the confidence of the one, and tameneſs of the other mutually increaſing; the reſt of the boys in the meanwhile ſurrounding and encouraging their companion. It is very remarkable, that this dolphin was followed by a ſecond, which ſeemed only as a ſpectator and attendant on the former; for he did not at all ſubmit to the ſame familiarities as the firſt, but only conducted him backwards and forwards, as the boys did their comrade. But what is farther ſurpriſing, and no leſs true than that which I have already related, is, this dolphin who thus played with the boys, and carried them upon his back, would come upon the ſhore, dry himſelf in the ſand, and as ſoon as he grew warm, roll back into the ſea. Octavius Avitus, deputy governour

of

of the province, actuated by an absurd piece of superstition, poured ᵇ some precious ointment over him as he lay on the shore: the novelty and smell of which made him retire into the ocean, and it was not till after several days that he was seen again, when he appeared dull and languid; however he recovered his strength, and continued his usual playful tricks. All the magistrates round the country flocked hither to view this sight; the entertainment of whom upon their arrival, and during their stay, was an additional expence, which the slender finances of this little community would ill afford; besides, that the quiet and retirement of the place was utterly destroyed. It was thought proper therefore to remove the occasion of this concourse, by privately killing the poor dolphin. And now, with what a flow of tenderness will you describe this affecting ᶜ catastrophe! and how

---

ᵇ It was a religious ceremony practised by the ancients, to pour precious ointments upon the statues of their gods: Avitus, it is probable, imagined this dolphin was some sea-divinity, and therefore expressed his veneration of him by the solemnity of a sacred unction.

ᶜ The overflowing humanity of Pliny's temper breaks out upon all occasions, but he discovers it in nothing more strongly than by the impression which this little story appears to have made upon him. True benevolence, indeed, extends itself thro' the whole compass of existence, and sympathizes with the distress of every creature capable of sensation. Little minds

how will your genius adorn and improve the interesting story! Tho', indeed, the subject does not require any fictitious embellishments; it will be sufficient to describe the fact in all its real circumstances. Farewel.

LETTER XXXIV. *To* Tranquillus.

ASSIST me in settling my doubts. I have not, I am told, a good manner of reading verses: as my talent lies chiefly in reciting orations, I succeed so much the worse, it seems, in poetry. I design therefore, as I am engaged to recite some poems to my particular friends, to make use of my freedman for that purpose. It is an instance, I own, of my treating them with little ceremony, that I assign this business to a person who is himself not very expert in it. However,

---

minds may be apt to consider a compassion of this inferiour kind, as an instance of weakness; but it is undoubtedly the evidence of a noble nature. Homer thought it not unbecoming the character even of a Hero, to melt into tears at a distress of this sort, and has given us a most amiable and affecting picture of Ulysses weeping over his faithful dog Argus, when he expires at his feet:

——αυταρ ο νοσφιν ιδων απομορξατο δακρυ.
Ρεια λαθων Ευμαιον——

Soft pity touch'd the mighty master's soul;
Adown his cheek the tear unbidden stole,
Stole unperceiv'd; he turn'd his head and dry'd
The drop humane.——
      Odys. xvii. Pope

ever, he will perform, I am sure, better than I can, provided his fears do not disconcert him; for he is as novel a reader as I am a poet. Now the question is, how it becomes me to behave while he is discharging my office; shall I sit in a fix'd and indolent posture, or follow him as he pronounces, with my looks, hands, and a low tone of applause; in the manner of a certain person whom you know? But I am apprehensive, I can appropriate my [a] gestures no better than I can read. I repeat it again therefore, you must extricate me out of this difficulty, and tell me truely, whether you think it more excusable to read ill, than to practise or omit any of the circumstances above-mentioned. Farewel.

LET-

---

[a] In the original it is called *saltatio*, which means a motion of the hands accommodated either to one's own, or another's elocution. Our language does not supply a proper word for this gesture, as indeed we have too little occasion to find the want of it; the *chironomic* art, so much studied by the ancients, being in the number of those which have been long since lost. But if the * *indoctae rusticaeve manus*, the aukward and unmeaning disposition of the hands, would have spoiled the noblest speech at Rome or Athens that Tully or Demosthenes, in all the warmth of their enlivening eloquence, ever delivered; it would not, perhaps, be time ill employed, if our modern orators would give a little more attention to the graceful management of those essential instruments of affecting elocution. This becoming art, so far as it was connected with masculine oratory, Pliny, most certainly, could not but be well skilled in: it is probable therefore, what he says in this place, alludes to this *affected manner* which certain authors of his time had fallen into, when they attended the rehearsal

of

* Quinctilian.

LETTER XXXV. *To* Appius.

I HAVE received your book, and return you my thanks, but am at present too much engaged to have time to read it; which, however, I impatiently wish to do. I have that high reverence for literature in general, and for your compositions in particular, that I think it a sort of profanation to approach them but with a mind entirely disengaged.—I extremely approve of your care in revising your works; but remember, correctness has its limits: too much polishing rather weakens than strengthens. Besides, this excessive delicacy, while it obstructs other pursuits, not only prevents any new attempts, but does not finish even what it has begun. Farewel.

of their own works; and that the whole turn of this epistle is ironical. This conjecture seems supported not only by the subject of the letter, which is scarce of importance enough to bear a serious enquiry; but also by the expression he sets out with, viz. *Explica æstum meum*, which seems to be of the ludicrous kind.

LETTER XXXVI. *To* Fuscus.

YOU desire to know in what manner I dispose of my time, in my summer villa at Tuscum? I rise just when I find myself in the humour, tho' generally with the sun; sometimes indeed sooner, but seldom later. When I am up, I continue to keep the shutters of my chamber-windows closed; as darkness and silence wonderfully promote meditation. Thus free and abstracted from those outward objects which dissipate attention, I am left to my own thoughts; nor suffer my mind to wander with my eyes, but keep my eyes in subjection to my mind: by these means they are not distracted with a multiplicity of external objects, and see nothing but what the imagination represents to them, If I have any composition upon my hands, this is the time I choose to consider it, not only with respect to the general plan, but even the stile and expression, which I revise and correct as if I were actually writing. In this manner I compose more or less as the subject is more or less difficult, and I find my memory able to retain it. I then call my secretary, and, opening the shutters, dictate to him what I have composed; after which I dismiss him for a little while, and then call him in again.

About

About ten or eleven of the clock (for I do not observe one fixed hour) according as the weather proves, I either walk upon my terrace, or in the covered portico; and there I continue to meditate or dictate what remains upon the subject in which I happen to be engaged. From thence I get into my chariot, where I employ myself as before, when I was walking or in my study; and find this changing of the scene refreshes and enlivens my attention. At my return, I repose myself; then take a walk, and after that, repeat aloud some Greek or Latin oration, not so much for the sake of strengthening my voice [a] as my digestion; tho' indeed the power of the voice at the same time is improved by this practice. I then walk again, am anointed, take my exercises, and go into the bath. At supper, if I have only my wife, or a few friends with me, some author is redde to us; and after supper, we are entertained either with music, or an interlude. When that is finished, I take my walk with my family, in the number of which, I am not without some persons of literature. Thus we pass our evenings in various conversation;

---

[a] By the regimen which Pliny here follows, one would imagine, if he had not told us who were his physicians, that the celebrated Celsus was in the number. That author expressly recommends reading aloud, and afterwards walking, as beneficial in disorders of the stomach; *Si quis stomacho laborat, legere clare debet; post lectionem ambulare, &c.* Celsi medic. L. 1. c. 8.

verfation; and the day, even when it is at the longeft, fteals imperceptibly away. Upon fome occafions I change the order in certain of the articles above-mentioned. For inftance, if I have ftudied longer or walked more than ufual; after my fecond fleep, and reading an oration or two aloud, inftead of ufing my chariot, I get on horfe-back; by which means I take as much exercife, and lofe lefs time. The vifits of my friends from the neighbouring villages claim fome part of the day; and fometimes, by an agreeable interruption, they come in very feafonably to relieve me when I am fatigued. I now and then amufe myfelf with fporting, but always take my tablets into the field, that if I fhould not meet with game, I may at leaft bring home fomething[b]. Part of my time too, is allotted to my tenants, tho' indeed not fo much of it as they defire: and I return from fettling their ruftic controverfies with a better relifh to my ftudies and more elegant occupations. Farewel.

[b] See B. 1. let. 6. and the note there.

LETTER XXXVII. *To* PAULINUS.

AS you are not of a disposition to expect from your friends, the common ceremonies of the world, when they cannot observe them without inconvenience to themselves; so I too warmly love you to be apprehensive you will take it unkind, my not waiting upon you on the first day of your entrance upon the consular office; especially as I am detained here by the necessity of letting my farms upon long leases. I am obliged to enter upon an entire new plan with my tenants: for, under the former leases, tho' I made them very considerable abatements, they have run greatly in arrear. For this reason several of them have, not only taken no sort of care to lessen a debt, which they found themselves incapable of wholly discharging; but even seized and consumed all the produce of the lands, in the belief that it would now be no advantage to themselves to spare it. I must therefore obviate this increasing evil, and endeavour to find out some remedy against it. The only one I can think of is, not to reserve my rent in money, but in kind, and so place some of my servants to overlook the tillage, and guard the stock; as indeed there is no sort of revenue more agreeable to reason, than what arises from the bounty of the soil, the seasons, and the climate. 'Tis true, this method will require great integrity and diligent attendance in the person I appoint my bailiff, and put me to the expence of employing many hands. However, I must hazard the experiment; and, as in an inveterate distemper, try every change of regimen. You see, it is not any pleasurable indulgence that prevents my attending you on the first day of your consulship. I shall celebrate it nevertheless, with as much festivity as if I were present, and pay my vows for you here, with sentiments of the warmest joy and congratulation. Farewel.

LETTER XXXVIII. *To* Saturninus.

YES, I sincerely applaud your friend Rufus; not because you desire me; but because I think he highly merits approbation. I have perused his very finished performance; to which, tho' my affection for the author added a considerable recommendation, yet it did not blind my judgement; for the malicious critic, is not, I trust, the only judicious reader. Farewel.

LETTER XXXIX. *To* Mustius.

IN compliance with the advice of the [a] Aruſpices, I intend to rebuild and enlarge the temple of Ceres, which ſtands upon my eſtate. It is indeed a very ancient fabric, and tho' extremely ſmall, yet upon a certain ſtated anniverſary is much frequented. On the 13th of September great numbers of people from all the country round aſſemble there: at which time many affairs are tranſacted, and many vows paid and offered; but there is no ſhelter for them againſt the inclemency of the weather. I think therefore, I ſhall perform an act both of piety and munificence, if at the ſame time that I build a beautiful temple, I add to it a ſpacious portico; the firſt for the ſervice of the Goddeſs, the other for the uſe of the people. I beg you to purchaſe for me four marble pillars, of whatever kind you ſhall think proper; as alſo a quantity of marble for laying the floor and incruſting the walls. You muſt likewiſe either buy a ſtatue of the Goddeſs, or procure one to be made; for, age has maimed,

in

---

[a] The buſineſs of the Aruſpices was, to examine the beaſts which were offered in ſacrifice, and from thence to foretel the ſucceſs of any enterprize.

in some parts, the ancient one of wood which stands there at present. With respect to the portico, I do not recollect there is any thing you can send me that will be serviceable; unless you will sketch me out a plan suitable to the situation of the place. It is not practicable to build it round the temple, because it is encompassed on one side by the river, whose banks are exceedingly steep; and on the other, by the high road. Beyond this road lies a very large meadow, in which the portico may be conveniently enough placed, opposite to the temple; unless you, who know so well how to conquer by art the inconveniencies of nature, can propose some better plan. Farewel.

LETTER XL. *To* Fuscus.

YOU are much pleased, I find, with the account I gave you in my former [a] letter, of the manner in which I spend the summer season at Tuscum; and desire to know what alteration I make in my method, when I am at Laurentinum in the winter? None, except abridging myself of my sleep at noon, and employing several hours both before day-light and after sun-set in study: but if

[a] See Let. 36. of this book, p. 196.

if any public bufinefs requires my early attendance at Rome, (which in winter very frequently happens) inftead of having interludes or mufic after fupper, I meditate upon what I have previoufly dictated, and by often revifing it in my own mind, fix it the more ftrongly in my memory. Thus I have given you a general fketch of my mode of life both in fummer and winter; to which you may add the intermediate feafons of fpring and autumn: in thefe, no part of the day is loft in fleep or diffipation as in fummer; fo fome time is gained for bufinefs or ftudy by the nights being fhorter than in winter. Farewel.

BOOK

BOOK the TENTH,

CONTAINING THE

LETTERS

OF

PLINY to TRAJAN,

AND OF

TRAJAN to PLINY.

THE LETTERS OF *PLINY.*

BOOK X.

LETTER ⁱ I. *To the Emperor* TRAJAN.

THE pious affection you bore, most sacred Emperor, to your august father; induced you to wish it might be late ere you succeeded him.

ᵃ The greater part of the following letters, were written by Pliny during his administration in the province of Bithynia. They are of a stile and character extremely different from those in the preceding collection; whence some critics have injudiciously infer'd, that they are the production of another hand; not considering, that the occasion necessarily required a different *manner.* In letters of business, as these chiefly are, *turn* and *sentiment* would be foreign and impertinent; politeness and elegance of expression being the essentials that constitute perfection in this kind: and in that view, tho' they may be less entertaining, they have not less merit than the former. But besides their particular excellence as letters, they have a farther recommendation as so many valuable pieces of history, by throwing a strong light upon the character of one of the most amiable and glorious princes in the Roman annals. Trajan appears throughout, in the most striking attitude that a sovereign can be placed; in the exertion of power to the

godlike

him. But the immortal Gods thought proper to hasten the advancement of those virtues to the helm of the commonwealth, which had already so successfully shared in the steerage[a]. May *you* then, and the world thro' your means, enjoy every prosperity worthy of your reign: to which let me add my wishes, most excellent Emperor, upon a private as well as public account, that your health and spirits may be preserved firm and unbroken.

LETTER II. *To the Emperor* TRAJAN.

YOU have occasioned me, Sir [b], an inexpressible pleasure, by deeming me worthy of enjoying the privilege which the laws confer on those who have

godlike purposes of justice and benevolence: and what one of the ancient historians has said of him, is here eminently verified, that "*he rather chose to be lov'd than flatter'd by his people.*" To have been distinguished by the favour and friendship of a monarch of so exalted a character, is an honour that reflects the brightest lustre upon our author; as to have been served and celebrated by a minister of Pliny's genius and virtues, is the noblest monument of glory that could have been raised to Trajan.

[a] Nerva, who succeeded Domitian, reigned but sixteen months and a few days. Before his death, he not only adopted Trajan, and named him for his successor, but actually admitted him into a share of the government; giving him the titles of *Cæsar, Germanicus,* and *Imperator.* Vid. Plin. Paneg.

[b] The translator has ventured to render the appellative *Dominus,* by that of *Sir,* not because he is satisfied with the strict propriety of the title, but as thinking it less exceptionable than any other our language affords That Pliny could not intend it as a title of royalty, seems evident from several passages in his panegyric, where whenever he uses it in that sense, he constantly includes in it a notion of tyranny. [Vid. Paneg. XLV. No. 4. LV. No. 7. LXXXV. No. 1.] Accordingly

have three children. For, altho' it was from an indulgence to the requeſt of the very worthy Servilianus, diſtinguiſhed by his affectionate attachment to your perſon, that you granted this favour; yet I have the ſatisfaction to find by the words of your reſcript, that you complied the more willingly, as his application was in my behalf. I cannot but look upon myſelf as in poſſeſſion of my utmoſt wiſh, after having thus received, at the entrance of your auſpicious government, ſo diſtinguiſhing a mark of your peculiar regard; at the ſame time that it conſiderably heightens my deſire of leaving a family behind me. I was not intirely without this deſire even in the late moſt wretched times ᶜ, as my two marriages will induce you to believe; but the Gods decreed it better, by reſerving every valuable privilege to the bounty of your generous diſpenſations. And indeed the ſatisfaction of being a father will be ſo much the greater to me *now*, that I can look forward to the enjoyment of that felicity in the full ſecurity of public freedom.

ingly we find Auguſtus refuſing the title of *Dominus*, as conveying an odious idea: *Ut maledictum & opprobrium ſemper exhorruit.* [Suet. in Aug. c. 53.] Beſides, the high ſtile of royalty would ill ſuit with that air of freedom and equality, which ſo remarkably diſtinguiſhes theſe letters of Pliny to Trajan; and the graceful ſimplicity of the Roman Conſul's addreſs, would be loſt in the ſervile forms of a modern courtier. But it appears from a paſſage in Seneca, that the Romans uſed the word *Dominus* as a general title of reſpect: *obvios, ſi nomen non ſuccurrit*, Dominos *appellamus.* [Sen. ep. 3.] And in that lower ſenſe, Pliny, it ſhould ſeem, here employs it.

ᶜ Alluding to the execrable reign of Domitian.

LETTER III. *To the Emperor* TRAJAN.

THE experience, most excellent Emperor, I have had of your unbounded generosity to me, in my own person, encourages me to hope I may be yet farther obliged to it, in that of my friends. Voconius Romanus (who was my inseparable companion and chamber-fellow at school) claims the first rank in that number; in consequence of which I petitioned your sacred father to promote him to the dignity of the Senatorial order. But the completion of my request is reserved to your goodness; for, his mother had not then advanced, in the manner the law directs, the four hundred thousand ª sesterces

---

ª In the original it is *sestertii quadringinties*, that is, about 320,000 l. sterling; a sum so immoderate, that the commentators have suspected (and with great reason) some errour must have crept into the text. Buchnerus and Gronovius imagine it should be read *quaterdecies* or *quadragies*; but this seems to be still carrying it much too high. The *census senatorius*, or the estate requisite to qualify a man to be a member of the senate, was, after different regulations, settled at length by Augustus at 1,200,000 sesterces, equal to about 9,600 l. of our money. It probably stood thus in Pliny's time; for as it appears by the 19th letter of the first book, that the *census equestris* was 400,000 sesterces, which is just the sum we find it at in the reign of Augustus; so it will not perhaps be unreasonable to infer from thence, that the *census senatorius* had not yet undergone any alteration since the time of that emperor, as they seem

sterces which she engaged to give him, in her letter to the late Emperor your father: This promise, however, by my advice she has since performed, having conveyed to him a sufficient estate in land, with all the necessary formalities. The difficulties therefore being removed which deferred the gratification of our wishes, it is with full confidence I venture to assure you of the merit of my friend Romanus, heighten'd and adorn'd as it is, not only by the liberal and polite arts, but by his extraordinary tenderness to his parents. It is to that virtue he owes the present liberality of his mother, as well as his immediate ᵇ succession to his late father's estate, and also his having been adopted by his father-in-law. To these personal quali-

---

seem to have borne a certain proportion to each other. For these reasons therefore, both the common reading, and the emendation of the above-mentioned critics, is rejected in the translation, and the conjecture of a late * editor adopted, who supposes it might be *quadringentorum millium*, 400,000 sesterces, or about 3,200 l: of our money. It has been questioned, whether by this *census senatorius* we are to understand the yearly income of the estate, or only the entire value of it: but the most generally received opinion is, that it means the latter, including both real and personal.

ᵇ Meaning, perhaps, that tho' he was under age when his father died, yet he had so much confidence in the prudence of Romanus, that he did not appoint him, as usual, a guardian by his will; but left him to the immediate possession of his estate.

* Gesnerus.

qualifications, the wealth and rank of his family give an increase of lustre; and I persuade myself it will be some additional recommendation, that I am a solicitor in his behalf. Let me then intreat you, Sir, to enable me to congratulate Romanus, on so desirable an occasion; and at the same time to indulge an earnest, and I hope laudable ambition of having it in my power to boast, that your favourable regards are extended, not only to myself, but to my friend.

LETTER IV. [xx.]^a *To the Emperor* TRAJAN.

WHEN by your gracious indulgence, Sir, I was appointed to preside at the ^b treasury of Saturn, I immediately renounced all engagements

^a *N. B.* The following letters to the 30th, are not ranged in the same order as they are placed in any of the Latin editions; the translator having taken the liberty of changing their situation, for the sake of bringing some letters together which throw a light upon each other. The figures included between this mark [ ] refer to the order in which they commonly stand.
^b The public treasure was kept in the temple of Saturn, where the spoils of the conquered nations were deposited. Julius Cæsar seized upon this temple in the time of the civil war; and what an immense wealth that plunder threw into his hands, may be judged by the elegant description which Lucan gives of the riches it contained:

——————— *tunc*

gagements of the bar, (as indeed, I never blended business of that kind with the functions of the state) that no avocations might call off my attention from the duties of that post to which I was promoted. For this reason, when the province of Africa petitioned the senate, that I might be permitted to undertake

---

———— *tunc conditus imo*
Eruitur templis, multis intactus ab annis
Romani census populi, &c.
LUCAN. iii. 155.

At length the sacred storehouse open laid,
The hoarded wealth of ages past display'd:
There might be seen the sums proud Carthage sent,
Her long impending ruin to prevent;
There heap'd the Macedonian treasures shone,
What great Flaminius and Æmilius won
From vanquish'd Philip, and his hapless son.
There lay what flying Pyrrhus lost, the gold
Scorn'd by the * patriot's honesty of old;
Whate'er our parsimonious sires could save:
What tributary gifts rich Syria gave;
The hundred Cretan cities ample spoil;
What Cato gather'd from the Cyprian isle.
Riches of captive kings by Pompey borne
In happier days his triumph to adorn,
From utmost India, and the rising morn;
Wealth infinite!
ROWE.

Pliny the elder has given a † particular valuation of this treasure which Cæsar seized, both in gold and silver plate, and in coin; the amount of which, according to Dr. Arbuthnot's computation, is,—1,093,979 l. 3 s. 4 d. But if there is no mistake in these sums, Cæsar did not take away by far so much as he brought in; for Plutarch relates ‡, that he placed at one time in the treasury, 65,000 talents; which, according to the same ingenious author's calculation, is equivalent to 12,593,750 pounds. Arb. Tab. 191.

* Fabricius. † Hist. Nat. l. 33. c. 3. ‡ In vit. Cæsar.

dertake their cause against Marius Priscus, I excused myself from that office; and accordingly my excuse was allowed. But when afterwards, the consul elect proposed, that the senate should apply to us again, and endeavour to prevail with us to yield to its inclinations, and suffer our names to be thrown into the * urn; I thought it most suitable to that tranquillity and good order which so happily distinguishes your times, not to oppose (especially in so reasonable an article) the will of that august assembly. And, as I am desirous that all my words and actions may receive the sanction of your exemplary virtue, I hope you will approve of my compliance.

---

* Other senators, as well as Pliny, had excused themselves, it seems, from undertaking the management of this cause; it was proposed therefore, that they should cast lots; which is the meaning of "suffering their names to be thrown into an "urn;" an urn being made use of in decisions of this kind. Accordingly, the lot fell upon our author, and his great friend the famous Cornelius Tacitus. See B. 2. let. 11. where there is a full account of this trial.

LETTER V. [xxi.] *The Emperor* TRAJAN *to* PLINY.

YOU acted as became a good citizen and a worthy senator, by paying obedience to the just requisition of that august assembly: and I have full confidence you will faithfully discharge the business you have undertaken.

LETTER VI. [iv.] *To the Emperor* TRAJAN.

HAving been attacked last year by a severe and dangerous illness, I employed a ª physician, whose care and diligence, Sir, I cannot sufficiently reward, but by your gracious assistance. I intreat you therefore to make him a ᵇ denizen of Rome; for as he is the freedman of a foreigner, he is, consequently, himself also a foreigner. His name is Har-

ª The physicians among the ancients were distinguished according to the particular branch of practice to which they confined themselves. The physician here mentioned, Pliny calls *Iatraliptes*, that is, one who applied external unctions.

ᵇ There was a difference between the *Jus Civitatis* and the *Jus Quiritium*; the former not extending to the same privileges as the latter, which comprehended whatever advantages a free native of Rome was entitled to: just in the same manner as with us there is a distinction between denization and naturalization.

Harpocras: his patroness (who has been dead a considerable time) was Thermuthis the daughter of Theon. I farther intreat you to bestow the full privileges of a Roman citizen upon Helia and Antonia Harmeris the freedwomen of Antonia Maximilla, a lady of great merit. It is at her desire* I make this request.

LETTER VII. [xxii.] *To the Emperor* TRAJAN.

I Return you thanks, Sir, for your ready compliance with my desire, in granting the complete privileges of a Roman, to the freedwomen of a lady to whom I am allied; and also for making Harpocras my physician a denizen of Rome. But when, agreeably to your directions, I gave in an account of his age and estate, I was informed by those who are better skilled in these affairs than I pretend to be, that as he is an Ægyptian, I ought to have previously obtained for him the freedom of Alexandria, before he was made free of Rome. I confess, indeed, that as I was ignorant of any difference in this case

between

---

* Pliny mentions his request to be at the particular desire of Maximilla, because nothing of this kind could legally be granted to a freedman, without the consent of his patron; a name which was given to the master of a slave whom he had emancipated.

between those of ᵃ Egypt and other countries, I contented myself with only acquainting you, that he had been manumized by a foreign lady, long since deceased. However, it is an ignorance I cannot regret, since it affords me an opportunity of receiving from you a double obligation in favour of the same person. That I may legally therefore enjoy the benefit of your goodness, I beg you would be pleased to grant him the freedom of the city of Alexandria, as well as that of Rome. And that your gracious intentions may not meet with any farther obstacles, I have taken care, as you directed, to send an account to your freedman of his age and possessions.

LETTER VIII. [xxiii.] *The Emperor* TRAJAN *to* PLINY.

IT is my resolution, in pursuance of the maxim observed by the princes my predecessors, to be extremely cautious in granting the freedom of the city of Alexandria; however, since you have obtained from me the freedom of Rome for your physician

---

ᵃ Upon what occasion the honour of this peculiar distinction was granted in favour of Alexandria does not appear; possibly it might be in gratitude to a country to which the Romans were so highly obliged, being supplied with the greatest part of their corn from Egypt. This city, founded by Alexander the great, was esteemed the most considerable in the world next to that of Rome. It is now called *Scanderick*.

sician Harpocras, I cannot refuse you this other request. You must let me know to what district he belongs, that I may give you a letter to my good friend Pompeius Planta, governour of Egypt.

LETTER IX. [v.] *To the Emperor* TRAJAN.

I Cannot express, Sir, the pleasure your letter gave me, by which I am informed that you have made my physician Harpocras a denizen of Alexandria; notwithstanding your resolution to follow the maxim of your predecessors in this point, by being extremely cautious in granting that privilege. Agreeably to your directions, I acquaint you that Harpocras belongs to the district of ª Memphis. I intreat you then, most gracious Emperor, to send me as you promised, a letter to your good friend Pompeius Planta, governour of Egypt.

As I purpose (in order to have the earliest enjoyment of your presence, so ardently wished for here) to go to meet you; I beg, Sir, you would permit me to extend my journey as far as possible.

ª One of the four governments of Lower Egypt.

LETTER X. [vi.] *To the Emperor* TRAJAN.

IN my late indisposition, I was greatly obliged, Sir, to Posthumius Marinus, my physician; and I cannot make him a suitable return, but by the assistance of your gracious indulgence. I intreat you then to make Chrysippus Mithridates and his wife Stratonica, (who are related to Marinus) denizens of Rome. I implore likewise the same privilege in favour of Epigonus and Mithridates, the two sons of Chrysippus; but with this restriction,[a] that they may remain under the dominion of their father, and yet preserve their right of patronage over their own freedmen. I farther intreat

---

[a] The extensive power of paternal authority, was (as has been observed in the notes above) peculiar to the Romans; but after Chrysippus was made a denizen of Rome, he was not, it should seem, consequentially entitled to that privilege over those children which were born before his denization. On the other hand, if it was expressly granted him, his children could not preserve their right of patronage over their own freedmen, because that right would of course devolve to their father, by means of this acquired dominion over them. The denization therefore of his children, is as expressly solicited as his own. But both parties becoming *Quirites,* the children by this creation, and not pleading in right of their father, would be *patres fam.* To prevent which, the clause is added, *ita ut sint in patris potestate;* as there is another to save to them their rights of patronage over their freedman, tho' they were reduced *in patriam potestatem.*

treat you to grant the full privileges of a Roman citizen to L. Satrius Abascantius, P. Cæsius Phosphorus, and Pancharia Soteris. This request I make with the consent of their patrons.

LETTER XI. [xxiv.] *To the Emperor* TRAJAN.

AFTER your late sacred father, Sir, had, in a noble speech, as well as by his own generous example, exhorted and encouraged the public to acts of munificence; I implored his permission to remove the several statues which I had of the former emperors, to [a] my corporation; and at the same time requested the liberty of adding his own to the number. For as I had hitherto continued them in the respective places wherein they stood when they came into my possession by several different inheritances; they were dispersed in distant parts of my estate. He was pleased to grant my request, and at the same time to give me a very ample testimony

of

---

[a] It is highly probable, upon comparing Let. 4. B. 3. and Let. 1. B. 4. that by the corporation here mentioned, Pliny means *Tifernum Tiberinum*, or *Citta di Castella*, as it is now called: which city had put itself under his patronage and protection.

of his approbation. I immediately therefore wrote to the Decurii, to desire they would allot a piece of ground, upon which I might erect a temple at my own expence; and they, as a mark of their honouring my design, offered me the choice of any site I should think proper. However, my own indisposition in the first place, and afterward that of your father, together with the duties of that employment with which you were both pleased to intrust me, prevented me from executing my intention. But I have now, I think, a convenient opportunity of making an excursion for that purpose, as my monthly [b] attendance ends on the first of September, and there are several festivals in the month following. My first petition therefore is, that you would permit me to adorn with your statue the temple I am going to raise; and the next (in order to the carrying on of my design with all possible expedition) that you would indulge me with leave of absence. It would ill become the sincerity I profess, were I to dissemble, that your goodness in complying with this desire, will at the same time be extremely serviceable to me in my own private affairs. It is

[b] Pliny enjoyed the office of treasurer in conjunction with Cornutus Tertullus. It was the custom at Rome for those who had colleagues to administer the duties of their posts by monthly turns. *Buchnerus.*

is absolutely necessary I should not defer any longer the letting of my lands in that province; for, besides that they amount to above ^c four hundred thousand sesterces, the season for dressing the vineyards is approaching, and *that* business must fall upon my new tenants. The badness of the weather likewise, for several years past, obliges me to think of making some abatements in my rents; which I cannot possibly settle unless I am present. I shall be indebted then to your indulgence, Sir, both as forwarding this public act of piety, and giving me the opportunity of settling my private affairs, if you will be pleased to grant me ^d leave to be absent for thirty days. I cannot limit a shorter time,

---

^c About 3,200l. sterling; the annual income of Pliny's estate in Tuscany. He mentions another near Comum in the dutchy of Milan, the yearly value of which does not appear. We find him likewise considering about the purchase of an estate, for which he was to give about 24,000l. of our money; but whether he ever completed that purchase, is uncertain. [See Book 3. let. 19.] This however we are sure of, that his fortunes were but moderate, considering his high station and necessary expences: [See Book 2. let. 4.] and yet, by the advantage of a judicious œconomy, we have seen him in the course of these letters, exercising a liberality, of which after-ages have furnished no parallel.

^d The senators were not allowed to go from Rome into the provinces, without having first obtained leave of the Emperor. Sicily, however, had the privilege to be excepted out of that law; as Gallia Narbonensis afterwards was, by Claudius Cæsar. Tacit. Ann. 12. c. 23.

time, as the town and the estate of which I am speaking, lie above an hundred and fifty miles from Rome.

LETTER XII. [xxv.] TRAJAN *to* PLINY.

YOU have given me many reasons both of a public and private nature, why you request leave of absence; but I need no other than that it is your desire: and I doubt not of your returning as soon as possible to the duty of an office, which so much requires your attendance. As I would not seem to check any instance of your affection towards me, I shall not oppose your erecting my statue in the place you mention; tho', in general, I am extremely cautious in giving any encouragement to honours of that kind.

LETTER XIII. [viii.] *To the Emperor* TRAJAN.

AS I am sensible, Sir, that the highest praise my actions can receive, is to be distinguished by so excellent a Prince; I beg you would be graciously pleased to add either the office of

Augur or [a] Septemvir (both which are now vacant) to the dignity I already enjoy by your indulgence; that I may have the satisfaction of publicly offering up those vows for your prosperity, from the duty of my office, which I daily prefer to the Gods in private, from the affection of my heart.

LETTER XIV. [xxvi.] *To the Emperor* TRAJAN.

HAVING safely passed the promontory of [b] Malea, I am arrived at [c] Ephesus with all my train, notwithstanding I was detained for some time by contrary winds: an information, Sir, in which, I trust, you will think yourself concerned. I design to pursue the remainder of my journey to the [d] province, partly in light vessels, and

---

[a] One of the seven priests who presided over the feasts appointed in honour of Jupiter and the other Gods: an office, as appears, of high dignity, since Pliny ranks it with the Augurship: of which see B. 4. let. 8. note [a].

[b] In the Peloponnesus; now called Capo Malca di-sant-Angelo. Catanæus observes, this passage was so dangerous, that the ancients had a proverb, *cum Maleam deflexeris, domesticos obliviscere*; "the man that sails by Malea must think no "more of his family."

[c] A city of Ionia, in Asia the less, still remaining.

[d] Bithynia, a province in Anatolia, or Asia the less, of which Pliny was appointed governour by Trajan, in the 6th year

and partly in post-chaises: for, as the extreme heats will prevent my travelling altogether by land, so the Etesian [e] winds, which are now set in, will not permit me to proceed entirely by sea.

LETTER XV. [xxvii.] Trajan *to* Pliny.

YOUR information, my dear Pliny, was very acceptable to me; as it is much my concern to know in what manner you arrive at your province. I well approve of your intention to travel either by sea or land, as you shall find most convenient.

LETTER XVI. [xxviii.] *To the Emperor* Trajan.

AS I had a very favourable voyage to Ephesus, so in travelling post from thence, I was extremely incommoded by the heats, which occasioned a fever, and detained me some time

---

year of his reign, A. Dom. 103. not as an ordinary Proconsul, but as that Emperor's own Lieutenant, with extraordinary powers. [See Dio.] The following letters were written during his administration of that province.

[e] A north wind in the Grecian seas, which rises yearly some time in July, and continues to the end of August; tho' others extend it to the middle of September. They blow only in the day-time. Varenius's Geogr. v. i. p. 513.

at [a] Pergamum. From thence, Sir, I took ship again; but being delayed by contrary winds, I did not arrive at Bithynia so soon as I hoped [b]. However, I have no reason to complain of this delay, since it did not prevent me from reaching the province in time to celebrate your birth-day: a circumstance which I consider as the most auspicious that could attend me. I am at present engaged in examining the finances of the [c] Prusenses, their disbursements and credits; and the farther I proceed in this affair, the more I am convinced of the necessity of my enquiry. Several considerable sums of money are owing to the city from private persons, which they neglect to pay upon various pretences; as, on the other hand, I find the public funds are, in some instances, very unwarrantably applied. This, Sir, I write to you immediately on my

---

[a] The famous Troy, situated in that part of Asia, which is now called Romania.

[b] The original adds, *id est, xv. Calend. Octobris*, which seems to have crept into the text from the marginal annotation of some glossarist: for as Pliny mentions the time of his arrival a little lower, there is no occasion for it in this place; and it is not agreeable to his usual elegant concisenefs, to repeat that circumstance twice in the same letter. Or perhaps here are two distinct letters run into one by the carelessness of the transcribers; the former ending with *Hæc*, &c. *in ipso ingressu meo scripsi*; the latter beginning with *Quintodecimo Calend. &c.*

[c] Prusa, a maritime city in Bithynia, supposed by some geographers to be the same which is now called *Cheris*; famous for producing great quantities of cherries, which take their name from thence.

my arrival. I entered this province on the 17th of [d] September, and found it in those sentiments of obedience and loyalty, which you justly merit from all mankind. You will consider, Sir, whether it would not be proper to send hither a surveyor; for I am inclined to think, much might be deducted from what is charged by those who have the conduct of the public works, if a faithful admeasurement were to be taken; at least I am of that opinion from what I have already seen of the accounts of this city, which I am now examining, with the assistance of Maximus.

LETTER XVII. [xxix.] TRAJAN to PLINY.

I Should have rejoiced to have heard that you arrived at Bithynia without inconvenience to yourself or any of your train; and that your journey from Ephesus had been as easy, as your voyage to that place was favourable. For the rest, your letter informs me, my dear Pliny, what day you reached Bithynia. The people of that province.

---

[d] In the sixth year of Trajan's reign, A. D. 103, and the 41st of our author's age: he continued in this province about 18 months. Vid. Mass. in vit. Plin. 129.

vince will be convinced, I perſuade myſelf, that I am attentive to their intereſt; as your conduct towards them will make it manifeſt, that I could have choſen no perſon more proper to ſupply my place. Your firſt enquiry ought, no doubt, to turn upon the ſtate of the public finances; for, it is but too evident they have been miſmanaged. I have ſcarce ſurveyors ſufficient to inſpect thoſe [a] works which I am carrying on at Rome, and in the neighbourhood; but perſons of integrity and ſkill in this art may be found, moſt certainly, in every province; ſo that you cannot be at a loſs in that article, if you will make due enquiry.

LETTER XVIII. [vii.] *To the Emperor* TRAJAN.

THO' I am well aſſured, Sir, that you, who never omit any opportunity of exerciſing your generoſity, are not unmindful of the requeſt I lately

---

[a] Among other noble works which this glorious Emperor executed; the Forum, or ſquare, which went by his name, ſeems to have been the moſt magnificent. It was built with the foreign ſpoils he had taken in war. The covering was intirely braſs, the porticos exceedingly beautiful, and the pillars of more than ordinary height and dimenſions. In the center of this Forum was erected the famous pillar which has been already deſcribed. See B. 8. let. 4. not. [a].

lately made you; yet since you have frequently, among many other instances of your indulgence, permitted me to repeat my solicitations, I renew them now on behalf of Accius Sura; and earnestly beseech you to honour him with the Prætorship, which is become vacant. Tho' his ambition is extremely moderate, yet the quality of his birth, the inflexible integrity he has preserved in a very narrow fortune, and, more than all, the felicity of your times, which encourages conscious virtue to claim your favour, induce him to hope he may experience it in the present instance.

LETTER XIX. [ix.] *To the Emperor* TRAJAN.

I Congratulate both you and the public, most excellent Emperor, upon the great and glorious victory you have obtained; so agreeable to the heroism of ancient Rome. May the immortal Gods give the same happy success to all your designs, that, under the administration of so many princely virtues, the splendour of the empire may shine

shine out, not only in all its former, but with additional lustre [a].

LETTER XX. [x.] *To the Emperor* TRAJAN.

MY lieutenant Servilius Pudens came to [b] Nicomedia, Sir, on the 24th of November; and by his arrival freed me, at last, from the anxiety of a very tedious expectation.

LETTER XXI. [xi.] *To the Emperor* TRAJAN.

YOUR generosity to me, Sir, was the occasion of my being connected with Rosianus Geminus, by the strongest ties; for he was my [c] Quæstor when I was Consul. His behaviour to me during the continuance of our offices, was highly respectful; and he has treated me ever since with so peculiar a regard, that besides the many obligations I owe

---

[a] It is probable the victory here alluded to, was that famous one which Trajan gained over the Dacians; some account of which has been given in the notes above. It is certain, at least, Pliny lived to see his wish accomplished; this Emperor having carried the Roman splendour to its highest pitch, and extended the dominions of the empire farther than any of his predecessors; after his death it began to decline.

[b] Now called Comedia, the capital city of Bithynia.

[c] See vol. i. p. 220, note [a].

I owe him upon a public account, I am indebted to him for the ſtrongeſt pledges of private friendſhip. I entreat you then to comply with my requeſt for the advancement of a worthy man, whom (if my recommendation has any weight) you will even diſtinguiſh by your particular favour; and whatever truſt you ſhall repoſe in him, he will endeavour to prove himſelf deſerving of a ſtill higher. But I forbear to enter into a more particular detail of his merit; being perſuaded, that his integrity, his probity, and his vigilance are well known to you, not only from thoſe high poſts which he has exerciſed in Rome within your immediate inſpection; but from his behaviour when he ſerved under you in the army. One thing, however, my affection for him inclines me to think I have not yet ſufficiently performed; and therefore, Sir, I repeat my intreaties that you will give me the pleaſure, as early as poſſible, of rejoicing in the advancement of my Quæſtor; or, in other words, of receiving an addition to my own honours in the perſon of my friend.

LETTER XXII. [xii.] *To the Emperor* TRAJAN.

I Know not, Sir, in what words sufficiently to express the joy I received, when I heard you had, in compliance with the request of my [a] mother-in-law and myself, granted Cœlius Clemens the Proconsulship of this [b] province after the expiration of his consular office; as it is a proof that your beneficence towards me graciously extends itself thro' my whole family. As I dare not pretend to make an equal return to those obligations I so justly owe you, I can only have recourse to vows; and ardently implore the Gods, that I may not be found unworthy of those favours, which you are repeatedly conferring upon me.

[a] Pompeia Celerina.

[b] Bithynia.

LETTER XXIII. [xiii.] *To the Emperor* TRAJAN.

I Received, Sir, a difpatch from your freedman Lycormas, defiring me, if any embaffy from [a] Bofphorus fhould come hither in the way to Rome, that I would detain it till his arrival. None has yet arrived; at leaft in the [b] city where I now am. But a courier paffing thro' this place from the king of [c] Sarmatia, I embrace the opportunity which accidently offers itfelf, of fending with him the meffenger which Lycormas difpatched hither; that you might be informed at once by his letter and the king's, of certain circumftances which it may be expedient, perhaps, that they fhould come to your knowledge at the fame time.

[a] Bofphorus Cimerius, now called *Vofpero*, in Krim Tartary.

[b] Nicea (as appears by the 15th Let. of this B.) a city in Bithynia now called Ifmich.

[c] Sarmatia was divided into European, Afiatic, and German Sarmatia. It is not exactly known what bounds the ancients gave to this extenfive region; however, in general, it comprehended the northern parts of Ruffia, Mufcovy, leffer Tartary, and the greateft part of the kingdom of Poland, &c.

LETTER XXIV. [xiv.] *To the Emperor* TRAJAN.

I AM informed by a letter from the king of Sarmatia, that some affairs have happened, of which it is requisite you should be immediately acquainted. In order therefore to expedite the dispatches which his courier was charged with to you, I granted him a warrant to make use of the public post[a].

[a] The first invention of public couriers is ascribed to Cyrus, who, in order to receive the earliest intelligence from the governors of the several provinces [*], erected post-houses throughout the kingdom of Persia, at equal distances, which supplied men and horses to forward the public dispatches. Augustus [†] was the first who introduced this most useful institution among the Romans, by employing post-chaises, disposed at convenient distances, for the purpose of political intelligence. The magistrates of every city were obliged to furnish [‡] horses for these messengers, upon producing a *diploma*, or a kind of warrant, either from the emperor himself, or from those who had that authority under him. Sometimes, tho' upon very extraordinary occasions, persons who travelled upon their private affairs, were allowed to avail themselves of these post-chaises. [See Let. 121. of this Book.] It is surprising they were not sooner used for the purposes of commerce and private communication. Louis XI. first established them in France, in the year 1474; but it was not till the 12th of Car. II. [‖] that the post-office was settled in England by act of Parliament.

[*] Cyrop. l. 8. p. 496. edit. Hutchinson.
[†] Suet. in vit. Aug. c. 49.
[‡] Plutarch. in vit. Galbæ.
[‖] Rapin, vol. 2. 662. fol. ed.

LETTER XXV. [xv.] *To the Emperor* TRAJAN.

THE embassador from the king of Sarmatia having remained two days, by his own choice, at Nicea, where he found me, I did not think it reasonable, Sir, to detain him any longer; not only because it was still uncertain when your freedman Lycormas would arrive, but as some indispensable affairs require my presence in a different part of the province. Of this circumstance I thought it necessary that you should be informed, because I lately acquainted you in a letter, that Lycormas had desired, if an embassy should come this way from Bosphorus, that I would detain it till his arrival. But I did not see there was any pretence of retarding him any longer; especially as the dispatches from Lycormas, which (as I have already mentioned) I was not willing to detain, would probably reach you some days sooner than this embassador.

LETTER XXVI. [xvi.] *To the Emperor* TRAJAN.

I Received a letter, Sir, from Apuleius, an officer in the troops stationed at Nicomedia, informing me that one Callidromus being arrested by Maximus and Dionysius, (two bakers, to whom he had hired himself) fled for refuge to your ª statue; that being brought before a magistrate, he declared he was formerly slave to Laberius Maximus; but being taken prisoner by ᵇ Susagus in Mœsia ᶜ, he was sent as a present from Decebalus to Pacorus king of Parthia, in whose service he continued several years, from whence he made his escape and came to Nicomedia. When he was examined before me, he confirmed this account;

ª Particular temples, altars, and statues were allowed among the Romans as places of sanctuary to slaves, debtors, and malefactors. This custom was introduced by Romulus, who borrowed it probably from the Greeks; but during the free state of Rome, few of these asylums were permitted. This custom prevailed most under the Emperors, till it grew so scandalous, that the Emperor Pius found it necessary to restrain those privileged places by an edict. See Lipsii excurs. ad Taciti Ann. 3. c. 36.

ᵇ General under Decebalus.

ᶜ A province in Dacia, comprehending the southern parts of Servia and part of Bulgaria.

account; for which reafon I thought it neceffary to ᵈ fend him to you. I fhould have fent him fooner, but I deferr'd his journey, in order to make an inquiry concerning a gem which he faid was taken from him, upon which was engraven the figure of Pacorus in his royal habit: I was defirous (if it could have been found) of tranfmitting this curiofity to you, with a fmall ingot of Parthian gold, which he fays he brought from thence out of the mines. I have fixed my feal to it, the impreffion of which is, a chariot drawn by four horfes.

LETTER XXVII. [xvii.] *To the Emperor* TRAJAN.

YOUR freedman and ᵉ procurator, Maximus, behaved, Sir, during all the time we were together, with great probity, attention, and diligence; as one ftrongly attached to your intereft, and ftrictly obfervant of difcipline. This teftimony I very willingly give him; and I give it with all the fidelity I owe to you.

ᵈ The fecond expedition of Trajan againft Decebalus, was undertaken the fame year that Pliny went governour into this province: the reafon therefore why Pliny fent this Callidromus to the Emperor, feems to be, that fome ufe might poffibly be made of him in favour of that defign.
ᵉ Receiver of the finances.

LETTER XXVIII. [xviii.] *To the Emperor* TRAJAN.

AFTER having experienced, Sir, in Gabius Bassus, who commands on the frontiers of [a] Pontica, the greatest integrity, honour, and diligence, as well as the most particular respect to myself, I cannot refuse him my best wishes and suffrage; and I give them to him with all that fidelity which is due to you. I have found him abundantly qualified by having served in the army under you; and it is owing to the advantages of your discipline, that he has learned to merit the honour of your approbation. The military and the people here, who have had abundant experience of his justice and humanity, rival each other in that glorious testimony they give of his conduct both public and private: and I certify this with all the sincerity you have a right to expect from me.

[a] Krim Tartary.

LETTER XXIX. [xix.] *To the Emperor* TRAJAN.

Nymphidius [a] Lupus, Sir, served with me in the army. He commanded a body of the auxiliary forces at the same time that I was military tribune: and it was from that connection my affection for him began. A long acquaintance hath since mutually endeared and strengthened our friendship. For this reason I did violence to his repose, and insisted upon his attending me into Bithynia, as my assessor in council. He most readily granted me this proof of his amity; and without any regard to the plea of age, or of retirement, he shared, and continues to share with me, the fatigue of public business. I consider his relations therefore as my own; in which number, Nymphidius Lupus, his son, claims my particular notice. He is a youth of great merit and indefatigable application; and in every view of his character, well worthy of so excellent a father. The early

[a] The text calls him *Primipilarem*, that is, one who had been *Primipilus*, an officer in the army, whose post was both highly honourable and profitable; among other parts of his office he had the care of the Eagle, or chief standard of the legion.

early proof he gave of his merit, when he commanded a regiment of foot, is a proof that he is equal to any honour you shall think proper to confer upon him; and it gained him the strongest testimony of approbation from those most illustrious personages Julius Ferox, and Fuscus Salinator. I will add, Sir, that I shall rejoice in any increase of dignity which he shall receive, as an occasion of particular satisfaction to myself.

LETTER XXX. *To the Emperor* TRAJAN.

I Request your determination, Sir, in a point wherein I am greatly doubtful: it is, whether I should place the public slaves [a] as centinels round the prisons of the several cities in this province (as has been hitherto the practice) or employ a party of soldiers for that purpose? On the one hand, I am afraid the public slaves will not attend this duty with the fidelity they ought; and on the other, that it will engage too large a body of the soldiery: in the mean while, I have joined a few of the latter with the former. I am apprehensive, however, there may be some danger that this method will occasion a general neglect of duty, as it will afford them

---

[a] Slaves who were purchased by the public.

them a mutual pretence of throwing the blame upon each other.

LETTER XXXI. Trajan *to* Pliny.

THERE is no occasion, my dear Pliny, to draw off any [a] soldiers in order to guard the prisons. Let us rather persevere in the ancient custom observed in this province, of employing the public slaves for that purpose: the fidelity with which they shall execute their duty will depend much upon your care and strict discipline. It is greatly to be feared, as you observe, if the soldiers should be mixed with the public slaves, they will mutually trust to each other, and by that means grow so much the more negligent. But my principal objection is, that as few soldiers as possible should be withdrawn from their standard.

[a] In the original it is *Commilitones*, "my fellow-soldiers:" an appellation which those Emperors who desired to be well with the army affected to use. Suetonius informs us, that Augustus would never employ that expression, as thinking it a condescension unbecoming his dignity; and neither suitable to the tranquillity of the times, nor to military discipline.

LETTER XXXII. *To the Emperor* TRAJAN.

Gabius Bassus, who commands upon the frontiers of Pontica, in a manner suitable to the respect and duty which he owes you, has been with me, Sir, for several days. As far as I could observe, he is a person of great merit, and worthy of your favour. I acquainted him with your order that he should be contented with ten [a] beneficiary soldiers, two horse-guards, and one captain, out of the troops which you were pleased to assign to my command. He assured me those would not be sufficient; and that he would write to you accordingly: for which reason I thought it proper not immediately to recall his supernumeraries.

[a] The most probable conjecture (for it is a point of a good deal of obscurity) concerning the *Beneficiarii*, seems to be, that they were a certain number of soldiers exempted from the usual duty of their office, in order to be employed as a sort of body-guards to the General. These were probably foot; as the *Equites* here mentioned were perhaps of the same nature, only that they served on horse-back. *Equites singulares Cæsaris, Augusti, &c.* are frequently met with upon ancient inscriptions, and are generally supposed to mean the body-guards of the Emperor.

LETTER XXXIII. Trajan *to* Pliny.

I Have received from Gabius Baffus, the letter you mention, acquainting me, that the number of foldiers I had ordered him was not fufficient: and for your information I have directed my anfwer to be hereunto annexed. It is very material to diftinguifh between what the exigency of affairs requires, and what an ambitious defire of power may think neceffary. As for ourfelves, the intereft of the public muft be our only guide: accordingly, it is incumbent upon us to take all poffible care, that the foldiers fhall not be abfent from their ftandard.

LETTER XXXIV. *To the Emperor* Trajan.

THE Prufenfes, Sir, having an ancient bath which lies in a ruinous ftate, defire your leave to repair it; but upon examination, I am of opinion it ought to be rebuilt. I think therefore, you may indulge them in this requeft, as there will be a fufficient fund for that purpofe, partly from thofe debts which are due from * private perfons

* See let. 28. of this book.

to the public, which I am now levying; and partly from the money they raise among themselves towards furnishing the bath with oil, which they are willing to apply to the carrying on of this building: a work which the dignity of the city, and the splendour of your times seem to render necessary.

LETTER XXXV. TRAJAN *to* PLINY.

IF the erecting of a public bath will not be too great a charge upon the Prusenses, we may comply with their request; provided, however, that no new tax be levied for this purpose, nor any of those taken off which are appropriated to necessary services.

LETTER XXXVI. *To the Emperor* TRAJAN.

I AM assured, Sir, by your freedman and receiver-general Maximus, that it is necessary he should have an additional party of soldiers assigned to him, besides the *beneficiarii*,[a] which by your orders I appointed to the very worthy Gemellinus. Those therefore which I found in his service I thought

---

[a] See let. 32. of this book in note.

thought proper he should retain, especially as he was going into ᵇ Paphlagonia in order to procure corn. For his better protection likewise, and because it was his request, I added two of the cavalry. But I beg you would inform me, in your next dispatches, what method you would have me observe for the future in points of this nature.

LETTER XXXVII. Trajan *to* Pliny.

AS my freedman Maximus was going upon an extraordinary commission to procure corn, I approve of your having supplied him with a file of soldiers. But when he shall return to the duties of his former post, I think two from you, and as many from his coadjutor, my receiver-general Verbius Gemellinus, will be sufficient.

ᵇ A province in the lesser Asia, bounded by the Black-Sea and the rivers Delafs and Casilirmar.

LETTER XXXVIII. *To the Emperor* TRAJAN.

THE very excellent young man Sempronius Cælianus having discovered two [a] slaves among the recruits, has sent them to me. But I deferred passing sentence till I had consulted you, the restorer and supporter of military discipline, concerning the punishment proper to be inflicted upon them. My principal doubt is, that altho' they have taken the military oath, they are not yet entered into any particular legion. I request you therefore, Sir, to inform me, what course I should pursue in this affair, especially as it concerns example.

[a] The Roman policy excluded slaves from entering into military service, and it was death if they did so. However, upon cases of great necessity this maxim was dispensed with; but then they were first made free before they were received into the army, excepting only (as Servius in his notes upon Virgil observes) after the fatal battle of Cannæ; when the public distress was so great, that the Romans recruited their army with their slaves, though they had not time to give them their freedom. One reason, perhaps, of this policy might be, that they did not think it safe to arm so considerable a body of men, whose numbers, in the times when the Roman luxury was highest, we may have some idea of, by the instance which Pliny the naturalist mentions of Claudius Isodorus, who at his death was possessed of no less than 4,116 slaves, notwithstanding he had lost great numbers in the civil wars. Plin. Hist. Nat. xxxiii. 10. Meursius de luxu Rom.

LETTER XXXIX. Trajan *to* Pliny.

SEmpronius Cælianus has acted agreeably to my orders, in sending such persons to be tried before you, as appear to deserve capital punishment. It is material, however, in the case in question, to enquire whether these slaves inlisted themselves voluntarily, or were chosen by the officers, or were presented as substitutes for others. If they were chosen, the officer is guilty; if they are proxies, the blame rests with those who deputed them; but if, conscious of the legal inabilities of their station, they presented themselves voluntarily, the punishment must fall upon their own heads. That they are not yet entered into any legion, makes no great difference in their case; for they ought to have given a true account of themselves immediately, upon their being approved as fit for the service.

LETTER XL. *To the Emperor* TRAJAN.

AS I have your permiſſion, Sir, to addreſs my-ſelf to you in all my doubts, you will not deem it below the dignity of your exalted ſtation, to deſcend to thoſe humbler affairs, which concern my adminiſtration of this province. I find there are in ſeveral cities, particularly thoſe of Nicomedia and Nicea, certain perſons who take upon themſelves to act as public ª ſlaves, and receive an annual ſtipend accordingly, notwithſtanding they have been condemned either to the mines, the ᵇ public games, or other puniſhments of the like nature. Having received information of this abuſe, I have been long debating with myſelf, how I ſhould act. On the one hand, to ſend them back to their reſpective puniſhments, (many of them being now grown old, and behaving, as I am aſſured, with ſobriety and modeſty) would, I thought, be proceeding againſt them too ſeverely; on the other, to retain convicted criminals in the public ſervice, ſeemed not altogether decent. I conſidered, at the ſame time,

---

ª See note let. 30. of this B.
ᵇ A puniſhment among the Romans, uſually inflicted upon ſlaves, by which they were to engage with wild beaſts, or perform the part of gladiators, in the public ſhews.

time, to support these people in idleness, would be an useless expence to the public; and to leave them to starve, would be dangerous. I was obliged therefore to suspend the determination of this matter, till I could consult with you. You will be desirous, perhaps, to be informed, how it happened that these persons escaped the punishments to which they were condemned. This inquiry I have also made, but cannot return you any satisfactory answer. The decrees against them were indeed produced; but no record appears of their having ever been reversed. It was asserted, however, that these people were pardoned upon their petition to the proconsuls, or their lieutenants; which seems likely to be the truth, as it is improbable that any person would have dared to set them at liberty without authority.

LETTER XLI. Trajan *to* Pliny.

YOU will remember you were sent into Bithynia, for the particular purpose of correcting those many abuses which appeared necessary to be reformed. Now none stands more in need of reformation, than that criminals, who have been sentenced to punishment, should not only be set

set at liberty (as your letter informs me) without any apparent authority, but even appointed to employments, which ought alone to be exercised by persons whose characters are irreproachable. Those therefore among them who have been convicted within these ten years, and whose sentence has not been reversed by proper authority, must be sent back to their respective punishments; but where more than ten years have elapsed since their conviction, and they are grown old and infirm, let them be disposed of in such employments, as are but few degrees removed from the punishments to which they were sentenced; that is, either to attend upon the public baths, cleanse the common shores, or repair the streets and highways; those being the offices to which such persons are usually sentenced.

LETTER XLII. *To the Emperor* TRAJAN.

WHile I was making a progress in a different part of the province, a most destructive fire broke out at Nicomedia, which not only consumed several private houses, but also two public buildings; the town-house and the temple of Isis, tho' they stood on contrary sides of the street. The occasion of its spreading thus wide, was partly owing to the violence of the wind,

and

and partly to the indolence of the people, who, it appears, stood fixed and idle spectators of this terrible calamity. The truth is, the city was not furnished with either ᵃ engines, buckets, or any single instrument proper to extinguish fires: which I have now however given directions to be provided. You will consider, Sir, whether it may not be adviseable to form a company of fire-men, consisting only of one hundred and fifty members. I will take care none but those of that business shall be admitted into it; and that the privileges granted them shall not be extended to any other purpose. As this corporate body will be restricted to so small a number of members, it will be easy to keep them under proper regulation.

ᵃ It has been generally imagined that the ancients had not the art of raising water by engines; but this passage seems to favour the contrary opinion. The word in the original is *Sipho*, which Hesychius explains (as one of the commentators observes) *instrumentum ad jaculandas aquas adversus incendia*; " an instrument to throw up water against fires." But there is a passage in Seneca which seems to put this matter beyond conjecture, tho' none of the critics upon this place have taken notice of it: *Solemus*, says he, *duabus manibus inter se junctis aquam concipere, & compressa utrimque palma in modum siphonis exprimere*, [Q. N. l. 2. 16.] where we plainly see the use of this *Sipho* was to throw up water, and consequently the Romans were acquainted with that art. The account which Pliny gives of the fountains at his Tuscan villa is likewise another proof.

LET-

LETTER XLIII. Trajan *to* Pliny.

YOU are of opinion it would be proper to establish a company of fire-men in Nicomedia, agreeably to what has been practised in several other cities. But it is to be remember'd, that societies of this sort have greatly disturb'd the peace of the province in general, and of those cities in particular. Whatever name we give them, and for whatever purpose they may be instituted, they will not fail to form themselves into factious assemblies, however short their meetings may be. It will therefore be safer, to provide such machines as are of service in extinguishing fires, enjoining the owners of houses to assist in preventing the mischief from spreading; and if it should be necessary, to call in the aid of the populace.

LETTER XLIV. *To the Emperor* Trajan.

AGreeably to the general notice we previously gave for that purpose, we have offered, Sir, our annual [a] vows, for your prosperity, in which that of the empire is essentially involved; imploring

---

[a] This was an anniversary custom observed throughout the Empire, on the 30th of December.

ing the Gods to grant that thefe yearly vows may never ceafe to be thus by public authority announced and offered.

LETTER XLV. Trajan *to* Pliny.

I Received the fatisfaction, my dear Pliny, of being informed by your letter, that you, together with the people under your government, have both difcharged and renewed your annual vows to the immortal Gods, for my health and happinefs.

LETTER XLVI. *To the Emperor* Trajan.

THE city of Nicomedia, Sir, have expended three millions three hundred and twenty-nine fefterces [a] in building an aquæduct; which, not anfwering the intent, the works are entirely fallen into ruin. They made a fecond attempt in another place, where they expended [b] two millions. But in this likewife they were difappointed; fo that after having been at an immenfe charge to no purpofe, they muft ftill be at a farther expence, in order to be accommodated with water. I have examined a fine fpring from whence the water may be conveyed over arches (as was attempted in their firft defign) in

fuch

---

[a] About 24,000 l. of our money.
[b] About 16,000 l. of our money.

such a manner that the higher, as well as level and low parts of the city may be supplied. There are but very few of the old arches remaining; the square stones, however, employed in the former, may be used in turning the new arches. I am of opinion part should be raised with brick, as that will be the easier and cheaper material. But that this work may not meet with the same ill success as the former, it will be necessary to send hither an architect, or some person skilled in the construction of this kind of waterworks. And I will venture to say, from the beauty and usefulness of the design, it will be an erection well worthy the splendour of your times.

LETTER XLVII. Trajan *to* Pliny.

CARE must be taken to supply the city of Nicomedia with water; and that business, I am well persuaded, you will perform with all the diligence you ought. But it is most certainly no less incumbent upon you to examine, by whose misconduct it has happened, that such large sums have been thrown away upon this attempt; lest they apply the money to private purposes, and the aquæduct in question, like the preceding, should be begun and afterwards left unfinished. You will let me know the result of your inquiry.

LETTER XLVIII. *To the Emperor* TRAJAN.

THE citizens of Nicea, Sir, are building a theatre, which, tho' it is not yet finished, they have already expended, as I am informed (for I have not examined the account myself) above ᵃ ten millions of sesterces; and, what is worse, I fear to no purpose. For, either from the foundation being laid in a marshy ground, or that the stones themselves were decayed, the walls are crack'd from

---

ᵃ About 80,000 l. of our money. To those who are not acquainted with the immense riches of the ancients, it may seem incredible that a city, and not the capital one, of a conquered province, should expend so large a sum of money upon only the shell (as it appears to be) of a theatre: but Asia was esteemed the most considerable part of the world for wealth; its fertilitity and exportations (as * Tully observes) exceeding that of all other countries. The ingenious Dr. Arbuthnot quotes an instance from Athenæus of Asiatic riches, which a man must be a tolerable arithmetician even to count. It is the value of the treasure of Sardanapulus, with which he made a funeral pile for himself and family when he was besieged by Arbaces king of the Medes. " Athenæus makes the value
" of the treasure of this pile to amount to 100,000,000 ta-
" lents, which reckoned in Babylonic talents, amounts to
" 16,953,125,000 l. This was only the value of the silver;
" there was besides a tenth part of that number of talents of
" gold, which if gold was reckoned in a decuple proportion,
" will just double that sum." *Arbuth. ant. coins*, p. 203.

* Orat. pro. Imp. Cn. Pomp.

from top to bottom. It deserves your consideration therefore, whether it would be best to carry on this work, or entirely discontinue it; or rather, perhaps, whether it would not be most prudent absolutely to destroy it: for the foundations upon which this building is raised, appear to me more expensive than solid. Several private persons have promised to erect at their own expence, some the portico, others the galleries above the [b] pit: but this design cannot be executed, as the principal fabric is at a stand. This city is also rebuilding upon a more enlarged plan, the [c] Gymnasium, which was burnt down before my arrival in the province. They have already been at some (and, I doubt, a fruitless) expence. The structure is not only irregular and ill-disposed, but the present architect (who it must be owned is a rival to the person who was first employed) asserts, that the walls, tho' they are [d] twenty-two feet thick, are not strong enough to support the superstructure, as their

[b] The word *Cavea* in the original, comprehends more than what we call the *Pit* in our theatres, as it means the whole space in which the spectators sate. These theatres being open at top, the galleries here mentioned were for the conveniency of retiring in bad weather.

[c] A place in which the athletic exercises were performed, and where the philosophers also used to read their lectures.

[d] The Roman foot consisted of 11 inches and 7 tenths of our standard.

their interstices are not cemented with mortar, nor are these walls strengthened with a testaceous covering.

The inhabitants of ᵉ Claudiopolis are sinking (I cannot call it erecting) a large public bath, upon a low spot of ground which lies at the foot of a mountain. The fund appropriated for the carrying on of this work, arises from the money which those honorary members you were pleased to add to their senate, paid (or at least are ready to pay whenever I call upon them) ᶠ for their admission. As I am afraid therefore the public money in the city of Nicea, and (what is infinitely more valuable than any pecuniary consideration) your benefaction in that of Claudiopolis, should be ill applied; I must desire you to send hither an architect to inspect, not only the theatre, but the bath; in order to consider whether, after all the expence which has already been laid out, it will be better to finish them upon the present plan, or reform the one, and remove the other: for otherwise we may perhaps throw away our future cost, by endeavouring not to lose what we have already expended.

ᵉ A city in Isauric, a province in Asia, situated at the foot of mount Taurus between Lyconia, Pamphilia, Cilicia, and the sea.

ᶠ The honorary senators, that is, such who were not received into the council of the city by election, but by the appointment of the Emperor, paid a certain sum of money upon their admission.

LETTER XLIX.   Trajan *to* Pliny.

YOU who are upon the spot, will best be able to consider and determine what is proper to be done concerning the theatre, which the inhabitants of Nicea are building; as for myself, it will be sufficient if you let me know your determination. With respect to the particular parts of this theatre which are to be raised at a private charge; you will see those engagements fulfilled, when the body of the building to which they are to be annexed, shall be finished.—These paltry Greeks are, I know, immoderately fond of Gymnastic diversions, and therefore, perhaps, the citizens of Nicea have planned a more magnificent fabric for this purpose than is necessary: however, they must be contented with such as will be sufficient to answer the use for which it is intended.

I entirely leave it to you to advise the Claudiopolitani as you shall think proper, with relation to their bath, which they have placed, it seems, in a very improper situation. As there is no province that is not furnished with men of skill and ingenuity,

ingenuity, you cannot possibly want architects; unless you think it the shortest way to procure them from Rome, when it is generally from Greece that they come to us.

LETTER L. *To the Emperor* TRAJAN.

WHEN I reflect upon the splendour of your exalted station, and the magnanimity of your spirit; nothing, I am persuaded, can be more suitable to both, than to point out to you such designs as are worthy of your glorious and immortal name, as being no less useful than magnificent. Bordering upon the territories of the city of Nicomedia is a most extensive lake; upon which the commodities of the country are easily and cheaply transported to the high road; but from thence, are conveyed in carriages to the sea-side, at great charge and labour. To remedy this inconvenience, will require, many hands; but upon such an occasion, they cannot be wanting; for the country, and particularly the city, is exceedingly populous: and one may assuredly hope, that every person will readily engage in a work which will be of universal benefit. It only remains then to send hither, if you shall think proper, a surveyor or an architect, in order to examine whether the lake lies above the level of the sea; the engineers of this province being of opinion that the former is higher by forty [a] cubits. I find there is in the neighbourhood of this place, a large canal, which was formerly cut by one of the kings of this country; but as it was left unfinished, it is uncertain whether the canal was for the purpose of draining the adjacent lands, or making a communication between the lake and the river. It is equally doubtful, whether the death of this Prince, or the despair of being able to accomplish the design, prevented its completion. If the latter, I am so much the more ambitious, for the honour of your illustrious character (and I hope you will pardon me the pride) that *you* may have the glory of executing, what [b] *kings* could only attempt.

LET-

---

[a] A Roman cubit is equal to 1 foot 5 inches $\frac{406}{1000}$ of our measure. *Arbuthnot's tab.*

[b] A commentator upon this passage thinks this a very extraordinary compliment; "As if, says he, an Emperor of Rome could not do more than a little king of Bithynia." But it is much more probable that this critic should be mistaken in his objection, than Pliny in his compliment; and tho' he will have it to be a *little* king, it is more reasonable to suppose our author meant some great king of Persia. Besides, *Imperator*, among the Romans, had not of itself any such high idea, as has been affixed to it in later times. The meaning therefore of this wish seems to be, that tho' Trajan was contented

LETTER LI. Trajan to Pliny.

THERE is something in the scheme you propose of opening a communication between the lake and the sea, which may, perhaps, tempt me to consent. But you must first carefully examine the situation of this body of water, what quantity it contains, and from whence it is supplied; lest by giving it an opening into the sea, it should be totally drained. You may apply to Calpurnius Macer for an engineer; as I will also send you from hence, some persons skilled in works of this nature.

LETTER LII. To the Emperor Trajan.

UPON examining the public expences of the city of Byzantium*, (which I find are extremely great) I was informed, Sir, that the appointments of the ambassadour, which they send yearly to you with their homage and the decree which

tented to be in title no more than General, [*Imperator*] yet in acts of public munificence he might be more than those who proudly stiled themselves kings.

* Now Constantinople.

which passes in the senate upon that occasion, amount to twelve[b] thousand sesterces. But knowing the generous maxims of your government, I thought proper to send the decree without the ambassadour; that at the same time they discharged their public duty to you, they might be eased in the manner of paying it. This city is likewise taxed with the sum of[c] three thousand sesterces towards defraying the expence of an envoy, whom they annually send to compliment the governour of Moesia: this expence I have also directed to be spared. I beg, Sir, you would deign either to confirm my judgment, or correct my error in these points, by acquainting me with your sentiments.

LETTER LIII. Trajan *to* Pliny.

I Well approve, my dear Pliny, of your having excused the Byzantines the expence of sending an ambassadour to me. I shall esteem their duty as sufficiently paid, tho' I only receive the act of their senate thro' your hands. The governour of Moesia must likewise excuse them, if they compliment him at a less expence.

[b] About 96 l. sterling.
[c] About 24 l. of our money.

LETTER LIV. *To the Emperor* TRAJAN.

I Beg, Sir, you would settle a doubt I have concerning your ª *Diplomas*; whether you think proper that those *Diplomas*, the dates whereof are expired, shall continue in force, and how long? For I am apprehensive I may thro' ignorance, either confirm such of these instruments as are illegal, or prevent the effect of those which are necessary.

LETTER LV. TRAJAN *to* PLINY.

THOSE Diplomas the dates whereof are expired, must by no means be made use of. For which reason it is an inviolable rule with me, to send new instruments of this kind into all the provinces before they are immediately wanted.

ª A diploma is properly a grant of certain privileges either to particular places or persons. It signifies also grants of other kinds; and it sometimes means * post-warrants, as, perhaps, it does in this place.

* See Let. xiv. of this book, in the notes.

LETTER LVI. *To the Emperor* TRAJAN.

UPON intimating, Sir, my design to the city of [a] Apamea, of examining into the state of their public funds and revenues; they told me they were very willing I should inspect their accounts, but that no Proconsul had ever yet perused them; as they had a privilege (and that of a very ancient date) of administring the affairs of their corporation in the manner they thought proper. I required them to draw up a memorial of what they then asserted, and I transmit it to you precisely as I received it; altho' I am sensible it contains several things foreign to the question. I beg you would honour me with your commands, how I am to act in this matter: for, I should be extremely sorry either to exceed, or to fall short of, the powers of my commission.

[a] A city in Bithynia.

LETTER LVII. Trajan *to* Pliny.

THE memorial of the Apameans annexed to your letter, saved me the necessity of considering the reasons they suggest, why the former Proconsuls forbore to inspect their accounts; since they are willing to submit them to your examination. Their compliance deserves to be encouraged; and they may be assured the enquiry you are to make in pursuance of my orders, shall be with a full reserve to their privileges.

LETTER LVIII. *To the Emperor* Trajan.

THE Nicomedians, Sir, before my arrival in this province, had begun to build a new Forum contiguous to their former, in a corner of which stands an ancient temple dedicated to the [a] *mother of the Gods.* This edifice must either be repaired, or removed; chiefly, because it is a much lower building than that very lofty one which
is

---

[a] Cybele, Rhea, or Ops, as she is severally called; from whom, according to the Pagan creed, the rest of the gods are supposed to have descended.

is now erecting. Upon enquiry whether any particular condition had been annexed to the dedication of this temple; I was informed that their ceremonies of dedication differ from ours. You will be pleased therefore, Sir, to consider whether a temple, which has not been consecrated according to our rites, may be removed [a] consistently with the reverence due to religion: for if there should be no objection from that quarter, the removal in every other respect would be extremely convenient.

LETTER LIX. Trajan *to* Pliny.

YOU may without scruple, my dear Pliny, if the situation requires it, remove the temple of the *mother of the Gods*, from the place where it now stands, to any other more commodious. You need be under no difficulty concerning the act of dedication; for the ground of a [b] foreign city is not capable of receiving that kind of consecration which is sanctified by our laws.

[a] Whatever was legally consecrated, was ever afterwards unapplicable to profane uses.

[b] That is, a city not admitted to enjoy the laws and privileges of Rome.

LETTER LX. *To the Emperor* TRAJAN.

WE have celebrated, Sir, (with those sentiments of gratulation which your virtues so justly merit) the day of your accession to the empire, which was also its preservation, imploring the Gods to preserve you in health and prosperity; for upon your welfare the security and repose of the world depends. I renewed at the same time the oath of allegiance at the head of the army, which repeated it after me in the usual form, the people of the province zealously concurring in the same oath.

LETTER LXI. TRAJAN *to* PLINY.

YOUR letter, my dear Pliny, was extremely acceptable, as it informed me of the zeal and affection with which you, together with the army and the provincials, solemnized the day of my accession to the empire.

LETTER LXII. *To the Emperor* Trajan.

THE debts which were owing to the public, are, by the prudence, Sir, of your councils, and the care of my administration, either actually paid, or are now recovering: but I am afraid the money must lie unemployed. For, as on one side, there are few or no opportunities of purchasing land, so on the other, one cannot meet with any person who is willing to borrow of the * public (especially at the interest of 12 *per cent.*) when they can raise money upon the same terms from private hands. You will therefore consider, Sir, whether it may not be adviseable, in order to invite responsible persons to take this money, to lower the interest; or if that scheme should not succeed, to place it in the hands of the Decurii, upon their giving sufficient security to the public. And tho' they should not be willing to receive it, yet as the rate of interest will be abated, the hardship will be so much the less.

---

* The reason why they did not chuse to borrow of the public at the same rate of interest which they paid to private persons, was (as one of the commentators observes) because in the former instance, they were obliged to give security; whereas in the latter, they could raise money upon their personal credit.

LETTER LXIII. Trajan to Pliny.

I Agree with you, my dear Pliny, that there seems to be no other method of facilitating the placing out of the public money, than by lowering the interest; the rate of which you will determine according to the number of borrowers. But to compel persons to receive it, who are not so disposed, when possibly they themselves may have no opportunity of employing it; is by no means consistent with the justice of my government.

LETTER LXIV. To the Emperor Trajan.

I Return you my warmest acknowledgments, Sir, that among the many important occupations in which you are engaged, you have condescended to be my guide in those points wherein I have consulted you: a favour which I must now again beseech you to grant me. A certain person presented himself to me with a complaint, that his adversaries, who had been banished for three years by the illustrious Servilius Calvus, still remained in the province: they, on the contrary, affirmed that Calvus had revoked their sentence, and produced his edict for that purpose: I thought it necessary therefore to refer the affair intirely to you. For, as I have your express orders not to restore any person who has been sentenced to banishment either by myself or others; so I have no directions with respect to those, who having been banished by some of my predecessors in this government, have by them also been restored. It is necessary for me, therefore, to beg you would inform me, Sir, how I am to act with regard to the above-mentioned persons, as also to others, who after having been condemned to perpetual banishment, have been found in the province without permission to return: for, cases of that nature have likewise fallen under my cognizance. A person was brought before me who had been sentenced to perpetual exile by the Proconsul Julius Bassus; but as I knew that the acts of Bassus, during his administration, had been rescinded, and that the senate had granted leave to all those who had fallen under his condemnation, of appealing from his decision at any time within the space of two years; I enquired of this man whether he had accordingly stated his case to the Proconsul? He replied, he had not. I intreat you therefore to inform me whether you would have him sent back into exile; or whether you think some more severe, and what kind of, punishment

punishment should be inflicted upon him, and such others who may hereafter be found under the same circumstances. I have annexed to my letter the decree of Calvus, together with the edict by which the persons above mentioned were restored, as also the decree of Bassus.

LETTER LXV. Trajan *to* Pliny.

I WILL let you know my determination concerning those exiles which were banished for three years by the Proconsul P. Servilius Calvus, and soon afterwards restored to the province by his edict, when I shall have informed myself from him of the reasons of this proceeding. With respect to that person who was sentenced to perpetual banishment by Julius Bassus, yet continued to remain in the province, without making his appeal, if he thought himself aggrieved, (tho' he had two years given him for that purpose) I would have him sent in chains to my [a] prætorian Prefects; for,

only

[a] These, in the original institution as settled by Augustus, were only commanders of his body-guards; but in the later times of the Roman empire, they were next in authority under the Emperor, to whom they seem to have acted as a sort of prime ministers.

only to remand him back to a punishment which he has contumaciously eluded, will by no means be a sufficient chastisement.

LETTER LXVI. *To the Emperor* TRAJAN.

WHEN I cited the judges, Sir, to attend me at a ªsessions which I was going to hold; Flavius Archippus claimed the privilege of being excused, as exercising the profession of a ᵇphilosopher. It was alledged by some who were present, that he ought not only to be excused from that office, but even struck out of the roll of judges, and remanded back to the punishment from which he had escaped by breaking his chains. At the same time a sentence of the Proconsul Velius Paullus was read, by which it appeared that Archippus had been condemned to the mines for forgery. He had nothing to produce in proof of this sentence having ever been reversed. He alledged, nevertheless, in favour of his restitu-
'tion,

ª The provinces were divided into a kind of circuits called *Conventus*, whither the Proconsuls used to go in order to administer justice. The judges here mentioned must not be understood to mean the same sort of judicial officers as with us; they were rather in the nature of our juries.

ᵇ By the imperial constitutions the philosophers were exempted from all public functions. *Catanæus*.

a petition which he presented to Domitian, together with a letter from that Prince and a decree of the Prusensians in his honour. To these he annexed a letter which he had received from you; as also an edict and a letter of your august father confirming the grants which had been made to him by Domitian. For these reasons, notwithstanding crimes of so atrocious a nature were laid to his charge, I did not think proper to determine any thing concerning him, without first consulting you; as it is an affair, which seems to merit your particular decision. I have transmitted to you, with this letter, the several allegations on both sides.

Domitian's LETTER to Terentius Maximus.

"FLavius Archippus the philosopher has pre-
" vailed with me to give an order for 600,000
" [a] sesterces to be laid out in the purchase of an
" estate for the support of him and his family, in the
" neighbourhood of [b] Prusias, his native country.
" Let

---

[a] About 4800 l. of our money.

[b] Geographers are not agreed where to place this city; Cellarius conjectures it may possibly be the same with *Prusa ad Olympum*, Prusa at the foot of Mount Olympus in Mysia, mentioned in Let. 85. of this book.

" Let this be done accordingly; and place that
" sum to the article of my benefactions."

From the same, to L. APPIUS MAXIMUS.

" I Recommend, my dear Maximus, to your
" protection, that worthy philosopher Archip-
" pus, whose moral conduct is agreeable to the
" principles of the philosophy he professes: and I
" would have you pay great regard to whatever he
" shall reasonably request."

The EDICT *of the Emperor* NERVA.

" THERE are some points, * Quirites,
" concerning which the happy tenour of my
" government is, I am persuaded, a sufficient in-
" dication of my sentiments; and a good prince
" need not give express declarations in matters
" wherein his intentions cannot but be universally
" understood. Every citizen in the empire will
" bear me witness, that I gave up my private
" repose to the security of the public, and in
" order that I might have the pleasure of dis-
" pensing new bounties of my own, as also of
" confirming those which had been granted by my
                                " predecessors.

* A general appellation given to the Roman people.

"predeceffors. But left the memory of him [b] who
"conferred thefe grants, or the diffidence of thofe
"who received them, fhould occafion any inter-
"ruption to the public joy; I thought it no lefs
"neceffary than it is agreeable to me to obviate
"thefe fufpicions, by affuring the perfons con-
"cerned of my indulgence. Let it not be thought
"that I fhall refcind either the public or private
"acts of any former Prince, in order to merit the
"credit of reftoring them; nor need any who
"have received the gratifications of imperial fa-
"vour, petition me to have them confirmed.
"Rather let them leave me at leifure for confer-
"ring new grants; under the affurance, that I am
"only to be folicited for thofe bounties which
"have not already been obtained, and which the
"happier fortune of the empire has put it in my
"power to beftow."

From the fame, to TULLIUS JUSTUS.

"HAVING publicly declared my refolution
"to confirm the edicts of my predeceffors,
"and even thofe alfo which may have been pre-
"vented by their deaths from being carried into
"effect; the directions contained in Domitian's
"refcript muft be obferved."

[b] Domitian.

LETTER LXVII. *To the Emperor* Trajan.

Flavius Archippus has conjured me, by all my vows for your prosperity, and by your immortal glory, that I would transmit to you the memorial which he presented to me. I could not refuse a request pressed upon me in *such* terms; however, I acquainted the prosecutrix with this my intention, from whom I have also received a memorial on her part. I have annexed them both to this letter; that by hearing, as it were, each party, you may the better be enabled to decide.

LETTER LXVIII. Trajan *to* Pliny.

It is possible that Domitian might be ignorant of the circumstances in which Archippus was, when he wrote the letter so much to that philosopher's credit. However, it is more agreeable to my disposition to suppose that prince designed

†　　　　　　　　　　　　　　　　　　　he

he should be restored to his former situation; especially since he so often had the honour of a statue decreed to him by those, who could not be [a] ignorant of the sentence pronounced against him by the Proconsul Paullus. But I do not mean to intimate, my dear Pliny, that if any new charge should be brought, you should be the less disposed to hear his accusers. I have examined the memorial of his prosecutrix, Furia Prima, as also that of Archippus himself, which you sent with your letter.

[a] In the text of all the editions it is *qui ignorabant*, but the reasoning seems to require the negative particle; though the commentators have passed over the passage without objection.

LETTER LXIX. *To the Emperor* TRAJAN.

THE apprehensions you express, Sir[a], that the lake will be in danger of being entirely drained, if a communication should be opened between that and the sea, by means of the river, are agreeable to that sagacity you so eminently possess; but I think I have found a method to obviate that inconvenience. A channel may be cut from the lake to the river, and a narrow slip of land left between them. By these means the water in the lake will not only be preserved and kept distinct from the river, but the same purposes will be answer'd as if they were united; for, it will be very easy to convey over that little intervening ridge, whatever goods shall be brought down by the canal. This is a scheme which may be pursued, if it should be found necessary; but I hope there will be no occasion to have recourse to it. For, in the first place, the lake itself is considerably deep; and in the next, by damming up a river which runs from it on the opposite side, and turning its course as we shall find expedient, the same quantity of water may still be retained. Besides, there are

several

---

[a] See letters 50 and 51 of this Book.

several little brooks near the place where it is proposed the channel shall be cut, which if skilfully collected, will supply the lake with water in proportion to what it shall discharge. But if you should rather approve of the channel's being extended farther, and cut narrower, and so conveyed directly into the sea, without running into the river; the reflux of the tide will return whatever it receives from the lake. After all, if the nature of the place should not admit of any of these schemes, the course of the water may be checked by sluices. These, however, and many other particulars, will be more skilfully examined into by the engineer, whom, agreeably to your promise, I hope you will send; for indeed, Sir, it is an enterprize well worthy of your attention and magnificence. In the mean while I have written to the illustrious Calpurnius Macer, in pursuance of your orders, to send me a skilful engineer proper for this occasion.

LETTER LXX. TRAJAN *to* PLINY.

IT is evident, my dear Pliny, that neither your prudence nor your care have been wanting in this affair of the lake; since, in order to render it of more general benefit, you have provided so many

many expedients againſt the hazard of its being drained. I leave it to your own choice to purſue which-ever of the ſchemes ſhall be thought moſt proper. Calphurnius Macer will furniſh you, no doubt, with an engineer, as artiſts of that kind are not wanting in his province.

LETTER LXXI. *To the Emperor* TRAJAN.

A Very conſiderable queſtion, Sir, in which this whole province is intereſted, has been lately ſtarted, concerning the ^d ſtate and maintenance of deſerted children. I have examined the conſtitutions of former Princes upon this head, but not finding any thing in them relating either in general or particular, to the Bithynians, I thought it neceſſary to apply to you for your directions: for, in a point which ſeems to require the ſpecial interpoſition of your authority, I could not content myſelf with following precedents. An edict of the Emperor Auguſtus (as pretended) was read to me concerning one Annia; as alſo a letter from Veſpaſian to the Lacedæmonians, and another from Titus to the ſame, with one likewiſe from him to the Achæans. At the ſame time ſome letters
from

^a That is, whether they ſhould be conſidered in a ſtate of freedom or ſlavery.

from Domitian were exhibited to me, directed to the Proconful Avidius Nigrinus, and Armenius Brocchus, together with one from that Prince to the Lacedæmonians: but I have not tranfmitted them to you, as well becaufe they were not correct (and fome of them too of fufpicious authority) as becaufe I imagine, the true copies are preferved in your archives.

LETTER LXXII. Trajan *to* Pliny.

THE queftion concerning fuch children who were expofed by their parents, and afterwards preferved by others, and educated in a ftate of fervitude, tho' born free, has been frequently difcuffed; but I do not find in the conftitutions of the Princes my predeceffors, any general regulation upon this head, extending to all the provinces. There are, indeed, fome refcripts of Domitian to Avidius Nigrinus and Armenius Brocchus, which ought to be obferved; but Bithynia is not comprehended in the provinces therein mentioned. I am of opinion therefore, that the claims of thofe who affert their right of freedom upon this principle, fhould be allowed without compelling them to purchafe their liberty by re-paying the money advanced for their maintenance.

LETTER LXXIII. *To the Emperor* TRAJAN.

Having been petitioned by certain persons to grant them the liberty (agreeably to the practice of former Proconsuls) to remove the relics of their deceased relations, suggesting that either their monuments were decayed by age, or ruined by the inundations of the river, or for other reasons of the same kind; I thought proper, Sir, knowing that in cases of this nature it is usual at Rome to apply to the college of Priests, to consult you, who are the sovereign of that sacred order, how you would have me act in this matter.

LETTER LXXIV. TRAJAN *to* PLINY.

It will be a hardship upon the provincials to oblige them to address themselves to the college of Priests, whenever they may have just reasons for removing the ashes of their ancestors. In this case therefore, it will be better you should follow the example of the governours your predecessors, and grant or deny them this liberty as you shall see reasonable.

LETTER LXXV. *To the Emperor* TRAJAN.

I Have enquired, Sir, at Prusa, for a proper place on which to erect the bath you were pleased to permit that city to build; and I have found one to my satisfaction. It is upon the site where formerly, I am told, stood a very beautiful fabric, but which is now entirely fallen into ruins. By fixing upon that spot, we shall gain the advantage of ornamenting the city in a part which at present is exceedingly deformed, and enlarging it at the same time without removing any of the present edifices; only rebuilding one which is fallen to decay. There are some circumstances attending this last structure, of which it is proper I should inform you. Claudius Polyænus bequeathed it to the emperor Claudius Cæsar, with directions that a temple should be erected to that Prince in the midst of a piazza; and that the remainder of the edifice should be let out in apartments. The city received the rents for a considerable time; but the piazza, together with the whole dome, partly by having been plundered, and partly by being neglected, is entirely gone to ruin, and there is now scarce any thing remaining but the ground upon which it stood. If you should think proper, Sir, either to give or sell this spot of ground to the city, as it lyes so conveniently for their purpose, they will receive the favour as the highest mark of your indulgence. I intend, with your permission, to place the bath in the vacant area, and to extend a range of porticos with seats, in that part where the former edifice stood. This new erection I design to dedicate to you, by whose bounty it will rise with all the elegance and magnificence worthy of your glorious name. I have sent you a copy of the will, by which, tho' it is incorrect, you will see, that Polyænus left several ornamental articles for the embellishment of this house; but these also are lost with all the rest: I will however make the strictest enquiry after them that I am able.

LETTER LXXVI. TRAJAN *to* PLINY.

I Have no objection to the Prusenses making use of the area together wih the untenanted house, which you say is fallen into ruins, for the situation of their bath. But is not sufficiently clear by your letter, whether the temple in the center of the piazza was actually dedicated to Claudius, or not; for if it were, it is still consecrated ground [a].

[a] And consequently by the Roman laws unapplicable to any other purpose.

LETTER LXXVII. To the Emperor TRAJAN.

I Have been preſſed by ſome perſons to take upon myſelf the cognizance of cauſes relating to claims of freedom by birth-right, agreeably to a reſcript of Domitian's to Minucius Rufus, and to the practice of former Proconſuls. But upon caſting my eye on the decree of the ſenate concerning caſes of this nature, I find it only mentions [a] the Proconſular provinces. I have therefore, Sir, deferred interfering in this affair, till I ſhall receive your commands how you would have me act.

[a] The Roman provinces in the times of the Emperors, were of two ſorts, and diſtinguiſhed by the name of the *Provinciæ Cæſaris*, and the *Provinciæ Senatus*. The *Provinciæ Cæſaris*, or Imperial provinces, were ſuch as the Emperor, for reaſons of policy, reſerved to his own immediate adminiſtration, or of thoſe whom he thought proper to appoint: The *Provinciæ Senatus*, or Proconſular provinces, were ſuch as he left to the government of Proconſuls, or Prætors, choſen in the ordinary method of election. [*Vid. Suet. in Aug.* c. 44. n. 1.] Of the former kind was Bithynia, at the time when our author preſided in that province. *Vid. Maſſon. vit. Plin.* p. 133.

LETTER LXXVIII. Trajan *to* Pliny.

IF you will send me the decree of the senate, which occasioned your doubt, I shall be able to judge, whether it is proper you should take cognizance of causes relating to claims of freedom by birth-right.

LETTER LXXIX. *To the Emperor* Trajan.

JUlius Largus, of the province of [a] Pontica, (a person whom I never saw, nor indeed ever heard his name till lately) in confidence, Sir, of your distinguishing judgment in my favour, has intrusted me with the execution of the last instance of his loyalty towards you. He has left me by his will, his estate upon trust, in the first place to receive out of it 50,000 sesterces [b] for my own use, and to apply the remainder for the benefit of the cities of [c] Heraclea and Tios, either by erecting some public edifice dedicated to your honour, or instituting Athletic games, as I shall judge proper.
These

[a] A province in Asia, bordering upon the black sea, and by some ancient geographers considered as one province with Bithynia.
[b] About 400 l. sterling.
[c] Cities of Pontus near the Euxine or black sea.

These games are to be celebrated every five years, and to be called *Trajan's games*. My principal reason for acquainting you with this bequest is, that I may receive your directions which of the respective alternatives to choose.

LETTER LXXX. Trajan *to* Pliny.

BY the prudent choice Julius Largus has made of a trustee, one would imagine he had known you perfectly well. You will consider then which of the alternatives will most tend to perpetuate the testator's memory, under the circumstances of the respective cities; and make your option accordingly.

LETTER LXXXI. *To the Emperor* Trajan.

YOU acted agreeably, Sir, to your usual consummate prudence, when you ordered the illustrious Calpurnius Macer to send a legionary centurion to Byzantium[a]: You will consider whether the city of Juliopolis does not also deserve the same attention; which, tho' it is extremely small, sustains very great burthens, and is so much the more exposed to oppressions, as it is less capable of resisting them. Whatever benefits you shall confer

[a] Constantinople.

confer upon that city, will in effect be advantageous to the whole country; for, it is situated at the entrance of Bithynia, and is the town thro' which all who travel into this province generally pass.

LETTER LXXXII. Trajan *to* Pliny.

THE circumstances of the city of Byzantium are such, by the great confluence of strangers to it, that I thought it incumbent upon me to honour it with a legionary centurion's guard, which was always granted to them in former reigns. But if we should distinguish the city of Juliopolis in the same manner, it will be introducing a precedent for many other towns, whose claim to that favour will rise in proportion to their want of strength. I have so much confidence, however, in your administration, as to believe you will omit no method of protecting them from injuries. If any person shall act contrary to the discipline I have enjoined, let them be instantly corrected; or if they happen to be soldiers and their crimes should be too enormous for immediate chastisement; I would have them sent to their officers, with an account of the particular misdemeanour you shall find they have committed: but if the delinquents should be on their way to Rome, inform me by letter.

LETTER LXXXIII. *To the Emperor* TRAJAN.

BY a law of ᵃ Pompey's concerning the Bithynians, it is enacted, Sir, that no person shall be a magistrate, or be chosen into the senate under the age of thirty. By the same law it is declared, that those who have exercised the office of magistrate, are qualified to be members of the senate. Subsequent to this law, the Emperor Augustus published an edict, by which it was ordained, that persons of the age of twenty-two should be capable of being magistrates. The question therefore is, whether those who have exercised the functions of a magistrate before the age of thirty, may be legally chosen into the senate by the ᵇ Censors? And if so, whether, by the same kind of construction, they may be elected senators, at the age which en-

---

ᵃ Pompey the Great having subdued Mithridates, and by that means greatly enlarged the Roman empire, passed several laws relating to the newly-conquered provinces, and, among others, that which is here mentioned; as Catanæus observes from Appian.

ᵇ The right of electing senators did not originally belong to the Censors, who were only, as Tully somewhere calls them, *Guardians of the discipline and manners of the city*; but in process of time, they engrossed the whole privilege of conferring that honour.

titles them to be magistrates, tho' they should not actually have borne any office? For, this custom, it seems, has hitherto been observed, and is said to be expedient; as it is rather more advantageous that persons of noble birth should be admitted into the senate, than those of Plebeian rank. The Censors elect having desired my sentiments upon this point, I was of opinion, that both by the law of Pompey and the edict of Augustus, they who had exercised the magistracy before the age of thirty, might be chosen into the senate: and for this reason; because the edict allows the office of magistrate to be undertaken before thirty, and the law declares, that whoever has been a magistrate, should be eligible into the senate. But with respect to those who never discharged any office in the state, tho' they were of the age required for that purpose, I had some doubt; and therefore, Sir, I apply to you for your directions. I have subjoined to this letter the heads of the law, together with the edict of Augustus.

LETTER LXXXIV. Trajan *to* Pliny.

I Agree with you, my dear Pliny, in your conftruction; and am of opinion that the law of Pompey is fo far repealed by the edict of the emperor Auguftus, that thofe perfons who are not under twenty-two years of age may execute the office of magiftrates, and be received into the fenate of their refpective cities. But I think that they who are under thirty years of age, and have not difcharged the function of a magiftrate, cannot, upon pretence that in point of years they were competent to the office, legally be elected into the fenate of their feveral communities.

LETTER LXXXV. *To the Emperor* Trajan.

WHILST I was difpatching at my apartments in Prufa [a], fome affairs, Sir, relating to the public, with an intention of leaving that city the fame day; Afclepiades, a magiftrate, informed me, that Eumolpus had appealed to me from a motion which Cocceianus Dion made in their fenate.

[a] At the foot of Mount Olymous.

nate. Dion, it seems, having been appointed supervisor of a public edifice, desired that it might be assigned ᵇ to the city in form. Eumolpus, who attended as counsel for Flavius Archippus, insisted that Dion should first be required to deliver in his accounts relating to this work, before it should be assigned to the corporation; suggesting that he had not performed his office in a requisite manner. He added at the same time, that in this building, in which your statue is erected, the bodies of Dion's wife and son are entombed ᶜ; and urged me to hear this cause in the public court of judicature. Upon my assenting to his request, and deferring my journey for that purpose; he desired a longer day in order to prepare matters for the hearing, and that I would try this cause in some other city. I appointed the city of Nicea: and accordingly having taken my seat on the tribunal, Eumolpus,

pretending

ᵇ This, probably, was some act whereby the city was to ratify and confirm the proceedings of Dion under the commission assigned to him.

ᶜ It was a notion which generally prevailed with the ancients, in the Jewish as well as Heathen world, that there was a pollution in the contact of dead bodies, and this they extended to the very house in which the corpse lay, and even to the uncovered vessels that stood in the same room. [*Vid. Pot. Antiq.* v. 2. 188.] From some such opinion as this it is probable, that the circumstance here mentioned of placing Trajan's statue where these bodies were deposited, was esteemed as a mark of disrespect to his person.

pretending not to be yet sufficiently prepared, moved that the trial might be again put off: Dion, on the contrary, insisted it should be now heard. They debated this point very fully on both sides, and entered a little into the merits of the cause; when being of opinion, that it was reasonable it should be adjourned, and thinking it proper to advise with you in an affair which was of consequence in point of example, I directed them to exhibit the articles of their respective allegations, in writing: for, I was desirous you should judge from their own express representations, of the state of the question between them. Dion promised to comply with this direction; as Eumolpus also assured me he would draw up a memorial of what he had to alledge on the part of the community. But he added, that being only concerned as advocate on behalf of Archippus, whose instructions he had already laid before me, he had nothing to charge with respect to the sepulchres. Archippus however, for whom Eumolpus was counsel here, as at Prusa, assured me he would himself present a charge in form with respect to this last article. But neither Eumolpus nor Archippus (tho' I have waited several days for that purpose) have yet performed their engagement: Dion indeed has; and I have annexed his memorial to this letter. I have inspected

spected the buildings in question, where I find your statue is placed in a library; and as to the edifice in which the bodies of Dion's wife and son are said to be deposited; it stands in the middle of an area surrounded with a colonade. Deign, therefore, I intreat you, Sir, to direct my judgment in the determination of this cause above all others, as it is a point to which the public is greatly attentive. And, indeed, it highly deserves a very mature deliberation, since the fact is not only acknowledged, but countenanced by many precedents.

LETTER LXXXVI. Trajan *to* Pliny.

YOU well know, my dear Pliny, that it is my fixed maxim not to render myself an object of terror, either by severe and rigorous measures of government, or by encouraging accusations of treason against the respect due to my person: you had no reason, therefore, to hesitate a moment upon the point, concerning which you thought proper to consult me. Without entering into the merits of the question, (to which I would by no means give any attention, tho' there were ever so many instances of the same kind) I recommend to your care the examining of Dion's accounts relating to the public works which he has finished;

finished; as it is a case in which the interest of the city is concerned, and as Dion neither ought, nor, it seems, does refuse, to submit to the examination.

LETTER LXXXVII. *To the Emperor* TRAJAN.

THE Niceans having, in the name of their community, conjured me, Sir, by all my hopes and wishes for your prosperity and immortal glory (an adjuration which is and ought to be most sacred to me) to present to you their petition; I did not think myself at liberty to refuse them: I have therefore annexed it to this letter.

LETTER LXXXVIII. TRAJAN *to* PLINY.

THE Niceans, I find, claim a right, by an edict of Augustus, to the estate of every citizen who dies intestate. You will therefore summon the several parties interested in this question, and with the assistance of Epimachus and Gemellinus, my Procurators (having duly weighed every argument that shall be alledged against the claim) determine as shall appear most equitable.

LETTER LXXXIX. *To the Emperor* Trajan.

MAY this and many succeeding birth-days be attended, Sir, with the highest felicity to you; and may you, in the midst of an uninterrupted course of health and prosperity, be still adding to the increase of that immortal glory, which your virtues justly merit!

LETTER XC. Trajan *to* Pliny.

YOUR wishes, my dear Pliny, for my enjoyment of many happy birth-days amidst the glory and prosperity of the republic, were extremely agreeable to me.

LETTER XCI. *To the Emperor* Trajan.

THE city of [a] Sinope is ill supplied, Sir, with water, which however may be brought thither from about sixteen miles distance, in great plenty and perfection. The ground indeed, near the source of this spring, is, for somewhat more than

[a] In the province of Pontica.

than a mile, of a very fufpicious and loofe nature; but I have directed an examination to be made (which will be effected at a fmall expence) whether it is fufficiently firm to fupport any fuperftructure. I have taken care to provide a fuitable fund for this purpofe, if you fhould approve, Sir, of a work fo conducive to the health and pleafure of this colony greatly diftreffed by a fcarcity of water.

LETTER XCII. Trajan *to* Pliny.

I Would have you proceed, my dear Pliny, in carefully examining, whether the ground you fufpect, is firm enough to fupport an aquæduct. For, I have no manner of doubt that it is proper the city of Sinope fhould be fupplied with water; provided their finances will bear the expence of a work fo conducive to their health and pleafure.

LETTER XCIII. *To the Emperor* Trajan.

THE free and confederate city of ª Amifus enjoys, by your indulgence, the privilege of being governed by its own laws. A memorial having

---

ª A colony of Athenians in the province of Pontica.

having been there prefented to me concerning a charitable [b] inftitution, I have fubjoined it to this letter, that you may confider, Sir, whether, and how far, this fociety ought to be licenfed or prohibited.

LETTER XCIV. Trajan to Pliny.

IF the prayer of the petition of the Amifeni which you have tranfmitted to me, concerning the eftablifhment of a charitable fociety, be agreeable to their own laws, which by the articles of alliance it is ftipulated they fhall enjoy, I fhall not oppofe it; efpecially if thefe contributions are employed, not for the purpofes of riot and faction, but for the fupport of the indigent. In other cities however, which are fubject to our laws, I would have all affemblies of this nature prohibited.

[b] The learned Cafaubon, in his obfervations upon Theophraftus (as cited by one of the commentators) informs us that there were at Athens and other cities of Greece, certain fraternities, which paid into a common cheft a monthly contribution towards the fupport of fuch of their members who had fallen into misfortunes; upon condition that if ever they arrived to more profperous circumftances, they fhould repay into the general fund the money fo advanced.

LETTER XCV. *To the Emperor* TRAJAN.

SUetonius Tranquillus, Sir, is a person of great probity and learning, as well as of noble birth. I was so much pleased with his disposition and manners, that I long since invited him into my family, as my constant guest and domestic friend; and my affection for him increased the more I discovered of his character. Two reasons concur to render the privilege [a] which the law grants to those

---

[a] By the law for encouragement of matrimony (some account of which has already been given in the notes above) those who lived batchelors, were declared incapable of inheriting any legacy by will; so likewise if being married, they had no children, they could not claim the full advantage of benefactions of that kind: [b] Thus Nævolus in Juvenal, very humorously urges his gallantries in his friend's family, as a meritorious piece of service which he had done him.

> *Nullum ergo meritum est, ingrate ac perfide, nullum,*
> *Quod tibi filiolus, vel filia nascitur ex me?—*
> *Jura parentis habes; propter* me *scriberis heres;*
> *Legatum* omne *capis, necnon & dulce caducum.*
>
> Sat. 9. v. 82, &c.

And ow'st thou nothing then, ingrate! to me,
That from my loins you sons and daughters see?
A parent's privilege by *me* you gain,
And the rich legacy in *full* obtain.

Pliny therefore alludes to this law, when he mentions the bounties of Tranquillus's deceased friends, as one reason why it was expedient for him to obtain the *jus trium liberorum*, viz. in order to entitle him to the full benefit of their several bequests.

[b] Lipsii excurs. in Tac. an.3. c. 24.

those who have three children, particularly necessary to him; I mean, the bounty of his friends, and the ill success of his marriage. Those advantages therefore, which nature has denied to him, he hopes to obtain from your goodness, by my intercession. I am thoroughly sensible, Sir, of the value of the privilege I am asking; but I know too I am asking it from one, whose gracious compliance with all my desires, I have amply experienced. How passionately I wish to do so in the present instance, you will judge by my thus requesting it in my absence; which I would not, had it not been a favour which I am more than commonly anxious to obtain.

LETTER CXVI. Trajan *to* Pliny.

YOU cannot but be perfectly sensible, my dear Pliny, how reserved I am in granting favours of the kind you desire; having frequently declared in the senate, that I had not exceeded the number which I assured that illustrious order I would be contented with. I have yielded, however, to your request; and have directed it to be inserted in my register, that I have conferred upon Tranquillus, on my usual conditions, the privilege which the law grants to those who have three children.

LET-

LETTER ᵃ XCVII. *To the Emperor* TRAJAN.

IT is a rule, Sir, which I inviolably obferve, to refer myfelf to you in all my doubts; for, who is more capable of removing my fcruples, or informing my ignorance? Having never been prefent at any trials concerning thofe perfons who are Chriftians, I am unacquainted not only with the nature of their crimes, or the meafure of their punifhment, but how far it is proper to enter into an examination concerning them. Whether therefore any difference is ufually made with refpect to the ages of the guilty, or no diftinction is to be obferved between the young and the adult; whether repentance intitles them to a pardon; or if a man has been once a Chriftian, it avails nothing to defift from his error; whether the very profeffion of Chriftianity, unattended with any criminal act, or only the crimes themfelves inherent

---

ᵃ This letter is efteemed as almoft the only genuine monument of ecclefiaftical antiquity relating to the times immediately fucceeding the Apoftles, it being written not above forty years at moft after the death of St. Paul. It was preferved by the Chriftians themfelves as a clear and unfufpicious evidence of the purity of their doctrines; and is frequently appealed to by the early writers of the church againft the calumnies of their adverfaries.

herent in the profession are punishable; in all these points I am greatly doubtful. In the mean while the method I have observed towards those who have been brought before me as Christians, is this: I interrogated them whether they were Christians: if they confessed, I repeated the question twice, adding threats at the same time; and if they still persevered, I ordered them to be immediately punished. For, I was persuaded, whatever the nature of their opinions might be, a contumacious and inflexible obstinacy certainly deserved correction. There were others also brought before me possessed with the same infatuation, but being [b] citizens of Rome, I directed that they should be conveyed thither. But this crime spreading (as is usually the case) while it was actually under prosecution, several instances of the same nature occurred. An information was presented to me without any name subscribed, containing a charge against several persons: these, upon examination, denied they were, or ever had been, Christians. They repeated after me an invocation to the gods, and offered religious rites

with

[b] It was one of the privileges of a Roman citizen, secured by the Sempronian law, that he could not be capitally convicted but by the suffrage of the people; which seems to have been still so far in force, as to make it necessary to send the persons here mentioned to Rome.

with wine and frankincense before your statue; (which for that purpose I had ordered to be brought together with those of the Gods) and even reviled the name of Christ; whereas there is no forcing, it is said, those who are really Christians, into any of these compliances. I thought it proper therefore, to discharge them. Some among those who were accused by a witness in person, at first confessed themselves Christians, but immediately after denied it; the rest own'd indeed they had been of that number formerly, but had now (some above three, others more, and a few above twenty years ago) renounced that errour. They all worshipped your statue and the images of the Gods, uttering imprecations at the same time against the name of Christ. They affirmed the whole of their guilt, or their errour, was, that they met on a certain stated day before it was light, and addressed themselves in a form of prayer to Christ, as to some God, binding themselves by a solemn oath, not for the purposes of any wicked design, but never to commit any fraud, theft, or adultery, never to falsify their word, nor deny a trust when they should be called upon to deliver it up: after which, it was their custom to separate, and then re-assemble, to eat in common a harmless meal. From this custom, however, they desisted

after

after the publication of my edict, by which, according to your commands, I forbade the meeting of any assemblies. In consequence of this their declaration, I judged it the more necessary to endeavour to extort the real truth, by putting two female slaves to the torture, who were said to officiate * in their religious functions; but all I could discover was, that these people were actuated by an absurd and excessive superstition. I deemed it expedient, therefore, to adjourn all farther proceedings, in order to consult you. For, it appears to be a matter highly deserving your consideration; more especially as great numbers must be involved in the danger of these prosecutions, which have already extended, and are still likely to extend, to persons of all ranks and ages, and even of both sexes. In fact, this contagious superstition is not confined to the cities only, but has spread its infection among the neighbouring villages and country. Nevertheless, it still seems possible to restrain its progress. The temples, at least, which were once almost

---

* These women, it is supposed, exercised the same office as Phœbe mentioned by St. Paul, whom he stiles Deaconess of the church of Cenchrea. Their business was to tend the poor and sick, and other charitable offices; as also to assist at the ceremony of female baptism, for the more decent performance of that rite: as Vossius observes upon this passage.

almost deserted, begin now to be frequented; and the sacred solemnities, after a long intermission are revived; to which I must add, there is again also a general demand for the victims, which for some time past had met with but few purchasers. From the circumstances I have mentioned, it is easy to conjecture what numbers might be reclaimed, if a general pardon were granted to those who shall repent of their error.

LETTER XCVIII. Trajan *to* Pliny.

THE method you have pursued, my dear Pliny, in the proceedings against those Christians which were brought before you, is extremely proper; as it is not possible to lay down any fixed rule by which to act in all cases of this nature. But I would not have you *officiously* enter into any enquiries concerning them. If indeed they should be brought before you, and the crime should be proved, they must be punished[a]; with this restriction

---

[a] If we impartially examine the present instance of the persecution of the Christians, we shall find it to have been grounded on the ancient constitution of the state, and not to have proceeded from an arbitrary or intolerant spirit in Trajan. The Roman legislature appears to have been early jealous of any innovation in point of public worship; and we find the magistrates,

striction however; that where the party denies he is a Christian, and shall make it evident that he is not by invoking our Gods; let him (notwithstanding any former suspicion) be pardoned upon h's

magistrates, during the old republic, frequently interposing in cases of that nature. Valerius Maximus has collected some instances to that purpose, [L. 1. c. 3.] and Livy mentions it as an established principle of the earlier ages of the commonwealth, to guard against the introduction of foreign ceremonies of religion. *Quoties* (says that excellent historian, speaking in the person of one of the consuls who is addressing himself to the people) *quoties hoc patrum avorumque ætate negotium est magistratibus datum, ut sacra externa fieri vetarent? Judicabant enim prudentissimi viri—nihil æque dissolvendæ religionis esse, quam ubi non patrio, sed externo ritu sacrificaretur.* [L. 39. c. 16.] It was an old and invariable maxim likewise of the Roman government, not to suffer any unlicensed assemblies of the people; as the reader must have observed by several of the preceding letters in this book: and to that fact Livy also bears witness; *Majores vestri* (says the historian) *ne vos quidem nisi quum,* &c. *forte temere coire noluerunt; & ubicunque multitudo esset, ibi et legitimum rectorem multitudinis censebant debere esse.* [L. 36. c. 25.]

The circumstance that attended the Christian assemblies being held at an unusual hour *(ante lucem,)* seems to have raised a surmise, that they were of the Bacchanalian kind. For it is extremely observable, that in the account which the Christians here give of the true design of their meeting, they justify themselves from the very crimes with which the Bacchanalians had been charged; intimating, it should seem, that they themselves had been taxed with the same: *se sacramento non ad scelus aliquod obstringere; sed ne furta, ne latrocinia, ne adulteria committerent, ne fidem fallerent,* &c. which runs exactly parallel with the accusation against the Bacchanalians, as it stands in Livy: *Nec unum genus noxæ, stupra promiscua,* &c. *sed falsi testes, falsa signa testimoniaque & indicia ex eadem officina exibant.* [Liv. l. 39. c. 8.]

Upon the whole then it appears evident, that these primitive Christians, deeply impressed with the evidence of the holy religion

his repentance. Informations without the accuser's name subscribed, ought not to be received in prosecutions of any sort; as it is introducing a very dangerous precedent, and by no means agreeable to the equity of my government.

LETTER XCIX. *To the Emperor* TRAJAN.

THE elegant and beautiful city of * Amastris, Sir, has, among other capital buildings, a most noble and extensive piazza. On one entire side of this structure runs, what is called indeed a river, but in effect is no other than a vile common shore, extremely offensive to the eye, and at the same time very unwholsome by its noxious vapours. It will be advantageous therefore in point of health, as well as ornament, to have it covered; which shall be done, with your permission: as I will take care, on my part, that money be not wanting for executing so noble and necessary a work.

gion they professed, nobly dared at all hazard to render themselves obnoxious, not particularly indeed to Trajan, but to the *antient* and *intolerant* laws of the state; by refusing to join in communion with the *established* worship, by assembling themselves without *legal* authority, and by holding their meetings at a suspicious hour of the night.

* Situated on the black sea, in the province of Pontus.

LETTER C. Trajan *to* Pliny.

IT is highly reasonable, my dear Pliny, if the water which runs thro' the city of Amastris is prejudicial to the health of the inhabitants, that it should be covered. I am well assured you will, with your usual attention, take care that the money necessary for this work shall not be wanting.

LETTER CI. *To the Emperor* Trajan.

WE have celebrated, Sir, with great joy and festivity, those votive solemnities which were publickly proclaimed as formerly, and renewed them the present year, accompanied by the soldiers and provincials; who zealously joined with us in imploring the Gods, that they would be graciously pleased to preserve you and the republick in that state of prosperity, which your many and great virtues, particularly your piety towards them, so justly merit.

LETTER CII. Trajan *to* Pliny.

IT was very agreeable to me to learn by your letter, that the army and the provincials joyfully seconded you with great unanimity, in those vows which you paid and renewed to the immortal Gods, for my preservation and prosperity.

LETTER CIII. *To the Emperor* Trajan.

WE have celebrated, with all the warmth of that pious zeal we justly ought, the day in which, by a very happy succession, the protection of the empire was delivered into your hands; recommending to the Gods, by whose gracious favour you received the sovereignty, the object of our public vows and congratulations.

LETTER CIV. Trajan *to* Pliny.

I Was extremely well pleased to be informed by your letter that you had, at the head of the soldiers and the provincials, solemnized my accession to the empire, with all due joy and zeal.

LETTER CV. *To the Emperor* TRAJAN.

Valerius Paulinus, Sir, having bequeathed to me the right [a] of patronage over all his freedmen, except one; I intreat you to grant the freedom of Rome to three of them. To desire you to extend this favour to all of them, would, I fear, be too unreasonable a trespass upon your indulgence; which, having amply experienced, I ought to be so much the more cautious in troubling. The persons for whom I make this request are, C. Valerius Æstiæus, C. Valerius Dionysius, and C. Valerius Aper.

LETTER CVI. TRAJAN *to* PLINY.

You act in a most worthy manner by consulting the interest of those persons whom Valerius Paulinus has confided to your trust; I cannot therefore but encourage you, as far as depends

---

[a] By the Papian law, which passed in the consulship of M. Papius Mutilus and Q. Poppeas Secundus. U. C. 761. if a freedman died worth a hundred thousand sesterces, (or about 800 l. of our money) leaving only one child; his patron, (that is, the master from whom he received his liberty) was entitled to half his estate; if he left two children, to one third; but if more than two, the patron was absolutely excluded. This was afterwards altered by Justinian, *Inst. l.* 3. *tit.* 8.

pends upon me, to lofe no time for that purpofe. I have accordingly granted the freedom of the city to fuch of his freedmen, for whom you requefted it, and have directed the patent to be regifter'd: am ready to confer the fame on the reft, whenever you fhall defire me.

LETTER CVII. *To the Emperor* TRAJAN.

P. Accius Aquila, captain of the fixth equeftrian cohort, requefted me, Sir, to tranfmit his petition to you, in favour of his daughter. I thought it would be unkind to refufe him this good office, knowing, as I do, with what patience and humanity you attend to the petitions of the foldiers.

LETTER CVIII. TRAJAN *to* PLINY.

I Have read the petition of P. Accius Aquila, captain of the fixth equeftrian cohort, which you fent to me; and in compliance with his requeft, I have conferred upon his daughter the freedom of the city of Rome. I fend you at the fame time the patent, which you will deliver to him.

LETTER CIX. *To the Emperor* TRAJAN.

I Request, Sir, your directions with respect to the recovering of those debts which are due to the cities of Bithynia and Pontus, either for rent, or goods sold, or for any other consideration. I find they have a privilege conceded to them by several Pro-consuls, of being prefer'd to other creditors; and this custom has prevailed, as if it had been established by law. Your prudence, I imagine, will think it necessary to enact some settled rule, by which their rights may always be secured. For the edicts of others, how wisely soever founded, are but feeble and temporary ordinances, unless confirmed and sanctioned by your authority.

LETTER CX. TRAJAN *to* PLINY.

THE right which the cities either of Pontus or Bithynia claim relating to the recovery of debts of whatever kind, due to their several communities, must be determined agreeably to their respective laws. Where any of those communities enjoy the privilege of being prefer'd to other creditors, it must be maintained; but where no such privilege prevails, it would not be just that I should establish one, in prejudice of private property.

LETTER CXI. *To the Emperor* TRAJAN.

THE folicitor to the treafury of the city of Amifis inftituted a claim, Sir, before me againft Julius Pifo of about 40,000 [a] denarii, which were prefented to him by the public above twenty years ago, with the confent of the general council and affembly of the city: and he founded his demand upon certain of your edicts, by which donations of this kind are prohibited. Pifo, on the other hand, afferted that he had confer'd large fums of money upon the community, and indeed, had expended in liberalities to them, almoft the whole of his eftate. He infifted upon the length of time which had intervened fince this donation, and hoped that he fhould not be compelled, to the ruin of the remainder [b] of his fortunes, to refund a prefent, which had

---

[a] About 1,166 l. Sterling.
[b] The tranflator has ventured to give this fenfe to *reliquæ dignitatis*. It is, he confeffes, a very uncommon, perhaps the fingle inftance of the word *dignitas* being ufed in that meaning; ftill, however, the context, together with the epithet which is joined with it, will, he trufts, clearly juftify him. There is nothing in the nature of this cafe to make it reafonable to fuppofe, that the dignity of Julius Pifo fhould be impeached: as little is it to be collected from any thing contained in this letter, or Trajan's anfwer. The adjective *reliqua* being added to *dignitas*, removes every fufpicion of its fignifying *honor* (as the ingenious French tranflator Monf. de Sacy, and his humble copier the Italian Tedefchi, have render'd it) for honour

fcarce

had been conferred upon him long since, in return for many good offices he had done to the city. For this reason, Sir, I thought it necessary to suspend giving any judgement in this cause, till I shall receive your directions.

LETTER CXII. Trajan *to* Pliny.

THO' by my edicts I have ordained, that no largesses shall be given out of the public money; yet, that numberless private persons may not be disturbed in the secure possession of their fortunes, those donations which have been made long since, ought not to be called in question or revoked. We will not therefore enquire into any thing that has been transacted in this affair so long ago as twenty years; for I would be no less attentive to secure the repose of every private man, than to preserve the treasure of every public community.

scarce admits of fractions, and there can be no remainder after a substraction of that kind. The truth, it should seem, is, that as the value of a man's estate was, among the Romans, a necessary qualification to render him capable of the dignities of the commonwealth, our author, by a figure of speech, puts *dignitas* for *facultas*; the consequent (to speak in the language of the grammarians) for the antecedent.

LETTER CXIII. *To the Emperor* TRAJAN,

THE Pompeian law, Sir, which is observed in Pontus and Bithynia, does not direct that any money shall be paid into the public chest by those who are elected into the senate by the Censors, for their admission. It has however been usual for such members as have been admitted into those assemblies, in pursuance of the privilege which you were pleased to grant to some particular cities, of receiving above their legal number, to pay [b] one or two [c] thousand denarii on their election. Subsequent to your grant of this privilege, the Proconsul Anicius Maximus ordained (tho' indeed his edict related to some few cities only) that those who should be elected by the Censors should also pay into the treasury a certain sum, which varied in different places. It remains therefore for your consideration, whether it would not be proper to settle a certain fixed sum for each member, who is elected into the council, to pay upon his admission; for, it well becomes you, whose every word and action deserves to be immortalized, to establish laws that shall endure for ever.

[b] About 29 l.   [c] and 58 l. Sterl.

LETTER CXIV. Trajan *to* Pliny.

I Can give no general directions applicable to all the cities of Bithynia, in relation to those who are elected members of their respective councils; whether they shall pay an honorary fee upon their admittance, or not. It seems best therefore, in the present case, (and indeed is ever the safest way) to leave each city to exercise its own peculiar laws. I think, however, the Censors ought to set the sum lower to those who are chosen into the senate contrary to their inclinations, than to the rest.

LETTER CXV. *To the Emperor* Trajan.

THE Pompeian law, Sir, allows the Bithynians to give the freedom of their respective cities to any person they think proper, provided he is not a foreigner, but native of some of the cities of this province. The same law specifies the particular causes for which the Censors may expel a member the senate; amongst which, that of being a foreigner is not mentioned. Certain of the Censors therefore have desired my opinion, whether they ought to expel a member if he should happen to be a foreigner. But I thought

thought it necessary to receive your instructions in this case; not only because the law, though it forbids foreigners to be admitted citizens, does not direct that a senator shall be expelled for the same reason, but because I am informed, that there is in every city several members of their respective senates, who are not natives. If therefore this clause of the law, which seems to be obsolete by long custom to the contrary, should be inforced, many cities, as well as individuals, will be thrown into great confusion. I have annexed the heads of this law to my letter.

LETTER CXVI. Trajan *to* Pliny.

YOU might well be doubtful, my dear Pliny, what reply to give to the Censors, who consulted you concerning their right to elect into the senate foreign citizens, tho' of the same province. The authority of law on one side, and long custom prevailing against it on the other, might justly occasion you to hesitate. The proper measure in this case will be, to make no change in what is past, but to suffer those senators who are already elected, though contrary to law, to keep their seats, to whatever city they may belong; and in all future elections, to pursue the direction of
the

the Pompeian law: for, to give it a retrospective operation, would necessarily introduce great confusion.

LETTER CXVII. *To the Emperor* TRAJAN.

IT is customary in this city upon any person's either taking the manly [a] robe; solemnizing his marriage: entering upon the office of magistrate, or dedicating any public work; to invite the whole senate, together with a considerable part of the commonalty to a feast, and distribute to each of the company one [b] or two denarii. I request you to inform me, whether you think proper this ceremony should continue to be observed, or how far you approve of it. For myself, tho' I am of opinion that upon certain occasions, especially those of public festivals, this kind of general invitations may be permitted; yet when they draw together a thousand persons, and sometimes more, it seems to be going beyond a reasonable number, and has somewhat the appearance of factious largesses.

[a] See vol. i. p. 22. note [a].
[b] About seven-pence of our money. The sum distributed upon these occasions, supposing the assembly to consist of a thousand persons, and two denarii given to each, would amount to about 58 l. sterl.

LETTER CXVIII. Trajan *to* Pliny.

IT is with reason you apprehend, that those public invitations, which extend to an immoderate number of people, and where the dole is distributed, not singly to a few acquaintance, but as it were to whole collective fraternities; may be turned to the factious purposes of ambition. But I appointed you to your present government fully relying upon your prudence, and in the persuasion that you would take proper measures for regulating the manners, and settling the peace of the province.

LETTER CXIX. *To the Emperor* Trajan.

THE Athletic victors, Sir, in the [a] Iselastic games, conceive that the stipend you have established for the conquerors, becomes due from the day they are crowned: for, it is not essential, they

---

[a] These games are called *Iselastic*, from the Greek word εισιλαυνω, *invehor*, because the victors, drawn by white horses, and wearing crowns on their heads, were conducted with great pomp into their respective cities, which they entered through a breach in the walls made for that purpose; intimating, as Plutarch observes, that a city which produced such brave and victorious citizens, had little occasion for the defence of walls. [*Catanæus.*] They received also annually a certain honourable stipend from the public.

they pretend, what time they were triumphantly conducted into their country, but *when* they merited that honour. On the contrary, when I consider the meaning of the term *Iselastic*, I am strongly inclined to think, that it is intended the stipend should commence from the time of their public entry. They likewise petition to be allowed the treat you give at those combats which you have converted into Iselastic, tho' their victories were gained before that change took place: for, it is but reasonable, they assert, that they should receive the reward in this instance, as they are deprived of it at those games which have been divested of the honour of being Iselastic, since their victories. But I am very doubtful, whether a retrospect should be admitted in the case in question, and a reward given, to which the claimants had no right at the time they obtained the victory. I beg therefore you would be pleased to direct my judgment in these points, by explaining the intention of your own benefactions.

LETTER CXX. Trajan *to* Pliny.

THE stipend appointed for the conqueror in the Iselastic games, ought not, I think, to commence till he makes his triumphant entry into his city; nor are the prizes, at those combats which I have thought proper to make Iselastic, to be extended to those who were victors before that alteration took place. With regard to the plea which these Athletic combatants urge, that they ought to receive the Iselastic prize at those combats which have been made Iselastic subsequent to their conquests, as they are denied it in the same case where the games have ceased to be so; it proves nothing in their favour: for, notwithstanding any new arrangement which has been made relating to these games, they are not required to return the recompence which they received prior to such alteration.

LETTER CXXI. *To the Emperor* Trajan.

I Have hitherto never, Sir, granted an order * for post-chaises to any person, or upon any occasion but in affairs that relate to your administration. I find myself however at present under a sort of necessity to break thro' this fixed rule. My wife

* See Let. xxiv. of this book, and the note there.

having received an account of her [b] grandfather's death, and being desirous to wait upon her [c] aunt with all possible expedition, I thought it would be unkind to deny her the use of this privilege; as the grace of so tender an office consists in the early discharge of it, and as I well knew a journey which was founded in filial piety, could not fail of your approbation. I should think myself highly ungrately therefore, were I not to acknowledge, that among other singular obligations which I owe to your indulgence, I have this in particular, that in confidence of your favour I ventured to do without consulting you, what would have been too late had I waited for your consent.

LETTER CXXII. Trajan *to* Pliny.

YOU did me justice, my dear Pliny, by confiding in my affection towards you. Without doubt, if you had waited for my consent to forward your wife in her journey by means of those warrants which I have entrusted to your care, the use of them would not have answered your purpose; as it was proper this visit to her aunt should have the additional recommendation, of being paid with all possible expedition.

[b] Fabatus.   [c] Hispulla.

THE END.

AN
ALPHABETICAL INDEX

OF THE

Persons NAMES to whom PLINY addresses the foregoing LETTERS.

N. B. *The Numeral refers to the Book, the Figure to the Epistle.*

A.

TO Acilius, iii. 14.
— To Albinus, vi. 10.
To Anianus, ii. 16.
— Antoninus, iv. 3, 18. v. 10.
— Apollinaris, ii. 9. v. 6.
— Ariston, v. 3. viii. 14.
— Arrianus, i. 2. ii. 11, 12. iv. 8, 12. vi. 2. viii. 21.
— Atrius Clemens, i. 10.
— Augurinus, ix. 8.
— Avitus, ii. 6.

B.

To Bassus, iv. 23.
— Bebius Hispanus, i. 24.

INDEX.

C.

To Caleſtrius Tiro, i. 12.
— Calphurnia, vi. 4, 7. vii. 5.
— Calvina, ii. 4.
— Calviſius, ii. 20. iii. 1, 19. v. 7. viii. 2. ix. 6.
— Caninius, ii. 8. iii. 7. vi. 21. vii. 18. viii. 4. ix. 33.
— Caninius Rufus, i. 3.
— Capito, v. 8.
— Catilius, iii. 12.
— Catilius Severus, i. 22.
— Celer, vii. 17.
— Celerina, ſee Pompeia.
— Cerealis, ii. 19. iv. 21.
— Clarus, ſee Septitius.
— Clemens, iv. 2.
— Coccia (and her huſband Spurinna) iii. 10.
— Colon, ix. 9.
— Corellia Hiſpulla, iii. 3. iv. 19. vii. 14. viii. 11.
— Cornelianus, vi. 31.
— Cornelius, ſee Fuſcus.
— Cornutus, vii. 21, 31.

E.

To Erucius, i. 16.

F.

To Fabatus, iv. 1. v. 12. vi. 12, 30. vii. 11, 16. 23, 32. viii. 10.
— Fabius, ſee Juſtus.
— Falco (Pompeius) i. 23. iv. 27. vii. 22. ix. 15.
— Ferox, vii. 13.
— Firmus, i. 19.
— Flaccus, v. 12.

To

INDEX.

To Fundanus (Minutius) i. 9. iv. 15. vi. 6.
— Fuscus, vii. 9. ix. 36, 40.

G.

To Gallus, ii. 17. iv. 17. viii. 20.
— Geminus, vii. 1, 24. viii. 5, 22. ix. 11, 30.
— Genialis, viii. 13.
— Genitor (Julius) ix. 17.

H.

To Hispanus, vi. 25.
— Hispulla, see Corellia Hispulla.

J.

To Julius, see Genitor.
— Junior, viii. 15. ix. 12.
— Junius, see Mauricus.
— Justut (Fabius) i. 11. vii. 2.

L.

To Lateranus, ix. 27.
— Lepidus, iv. 7.
— Lucinius, see Sura.
— Lupercus, ii. 5. ix. 26.

M.

To Macrinus, ii. 7. iii. 4. vii. 6, 10. viii. 17. ix. 4.
— Macer, iii. 5. v. 18. vi. 24.
— Mamilianus, ix. 16, 25.
— Marcellinus, v. 16. viii. 23.
— Mauricus (Junius) i. 14. ii. 18. vi. 14, 15.

INDEX.

To Maximus, ii. 14. iii. 2, 20. iv. 20, 25. v. 5.
    vi. 11, 34. vii. 26. viii. 19, 24. ix. 1, 23.
— Minucius, vii. 12.
— Minutianus, iii. 9. iv. 11. viii. 12.
— Minutius, see Fundanus.
— Montanus, vii. 29. viii. 6.
— Mustius, ix. 39.

N.

To Naso, iv. 6.
— Nepos, ii. 3. iii. 16. iv. 26. vi. 19.

O.

To Octavius Rufus, i. 7. ii. 10.
— Oppius, ix. 35.

P.

To Paternus, i. 21. iv. 14. viii. 16.
— Paulinus, ii. 2. iv. 16. v. 19. ix. 3, 37.
— Pompeia Celerina, i. 4.
— Pompeius, see Falco, and Saturninus.
— Pontius, v. 15. vi. 28. vii. 4.
— Præsens, vii. 3.
— Priscus, ii. 13. iii. 21. vi. 8. vii. 8, 19.
— Proculus, iii. 15.

Q.

To Quadratus, vi. 29. ix. 13.
— Quintilian, vi. 32.

INDEX.

R.

To Restitutus, vi. 17.
— Romanus, see Voconius.
— Rufus, vi. 22. v. 21. vii. 25.
— Rufinus, viii. 18.
— Rufo, ix. 19.
— Rusticus, ix. 29.

S.

To Sabinus, iv. 10. vi. 18. ix. 2, 18.
— Sabinianus, ix. 21, 24.
— Sardus, ix. 31.
— Saturninus (Pompeius) i. 8. v. 9. vii. 15. ix. 38.
— Scaurus, v. 13.
— Septitius, i. 1. vii. 28. viii. 1.
— Septitius Claurus, i. 15.
— Servianus, iii. 17. vi. 26.
— Severus, iii. 6, 18. iv. 28. v. 1. vi. 27. ix. 22.
— Sosius Senecio, i. 13.
— Sossius, iv. 4.
— Sparsus, iv. 5. viii. 3.
— Spurinna, iii. 10. v. 17.
— Sura (Licinius) iv. 30. vii. 27.
— Suetonius, see Tranquillus.

T.

To Tacitus (Cornelius) i. 6, 20. iv. 13. vi. 9. 16, 20. vii. 20, 33. viii. 7. ix. 10, 14.
— Tiro, vi. 1, 22. ix. 5.
— Titianus (Cornelius) i. 17. ix. 32.
— Tranquillus, i. 18. iii. 8. v. 2. ix. 34.
— Triarius, vi. 23.

V. To

INDEX.
V.

To Valens, iv. 24.
— Valerianus, ii. 15. v. 4, 14.
— Venator, ix. 20.
— Verus, vi. 3.
— Voconius (Romanus) i. 5. ii. 1. iii. 13. iv. 29. vi. 15, 33. viii. 8. ix. 7, 28.
— Urſus, iv. 9. v. 20. vi. 5, 13. viii. 9.

FINIS.

ERRATA, Vol. II.

Page 2. l. 3. after *hope*, add *that*.
    5. l. 2. for *seclude*, r. *wrap*.
  17. l. 2. after *orators*, add *were*.
  22. l. 10. for *your*, r. *you*.
  31. l. 5. for *pen*, r. *pencil*.
  88. l. 4. for *pen*, r. *pencil*.
112. l. ult. for *equitable*, r. *just*.
147. l. 4. after *asked*, dele *for*.
159. l. 8. for *papers*, r. *accounts*.
167. l. 1. for *shewn*, r. *fallen*.
189. l. 19. for *hither*, r. *thither*.
203. l. 10. after *thefe*, add *as*.

www.ingramcontent.com/pod-product-compliance
Lightning Source LLC
Chambersburg PA
CBHW021209230426
43667CB00006B/623